# Florida's Frogs, Toads, and Other Amphibians

UNIVERSITY PRESS OF FLORIDA

Florida A&M University, Tallahassee
Florida Atlantic University, Boca Raton
Florida Gulf Coast University, Ft. Myers
Florida International University, Miami
Florida State University, Tallahassee
New College of Florida, Sarasota
University of Central Florida, Orlando
University of Florida, Gainesville
University of North Florida, Jacksonville
University of South Florida, Tampa
University of West Florida, Pensacola

# Florida's Frogs, Toads, and Other Amphibians

~~~~~~~~~~~~~~~~

A Guide to Their Identification and Habits

R. D. BARTLETT AND PATRICIA P. BARTLETT

University Press of Florida
Gainesville · Tallahassee · Tampa · Boca Raton
Pensacola · Orlando · Miami · Jacksonville · Ft. Myers · Sarasota

16  15  14  13  12  11   6  5  4  3  2  1

Library of Congress Cataloging-in-Publication Data
Bartlett, Richard D., 1938–
Florida's frogs, toads, and other amphibians : a guide to their identification
and habits / R. D. Bartlett and Patricia P. Bartlett.
p. cm.
Includes bibliographical references and index.
ISBN 978-0-8130-3669-4 (alk. paper)
1. Amphibians—Florida—Identification. I. Bartlett, Patricia Pope, 1949–
II. Title.
QL653.F6B374    2011
597.8—dc22      2011011280

The University Press of Florida is the scholarly publishing agency for the State
University System of Florida, comprising Florida A&M University, Florida
Atlantic University, Florida Gulf Coast University, Florida International Uni-
versity, Florida State University, New College of Florida, University of Central
Florida, University of Florida, University of North Florida, University of South
Florida, and University of West Florida.

University Press of Florida
15 Northwest 15th Street
Gainesville, FL 32611-2079
http://www.upf.com

# Contents

# Preface

Although the reptiles of the state of Florida are well known to herpe-tologists, herpetoculturists, field biologists, and field herpers, for most folks the whys and wherefores of the amphibians—in fact the amphibians themselves—remain more enigmatic. And perhaps this is understandable. Amphibians by nature are quite reclusive, avoiding the sunny exposed locales and sun-warmed roadways that attract reptiles.

Of the more than 230 species and subspecies of reptiles and amphibians now found in Florida, 68 are amphibians. Of these, only a comparative handful are alien species, and of that handful only 3 species—the cane toad, the greenhouse frog, and the Cuban treefrog—could be considered firmly established. Two additional forms, the Australian great green treefrog and the Puerto Rican coqui, have been found with some regularity, but whether they are truly established is questionable.

Despite decades of seemingly unfettered population growth and corresponding habitat destruction and modification, there remain within the state of Florida myriad diverse (though often fragmented) habitats. These may be as specialized as the sand pine and rosemary scrub habitats of the Lake Wales Ridge (and other ridges) or as general as flooded roadside ditches. Amphibians and reptiles are found in all these habitats. Some species, such as the Florida bog frog, the gopher frog, and the seal salamander, are specialized and of very local distribution. Others such as the southern toad, the green treefrog, and the greater siren are less specialized and may be found over the entire state.

Come with us as we tour the habitats and look at each Floridian species and subspecies of amphibian—the frogs, toads, treefrogs, salamanders and newts, both native and introduced, in detail.

# Introduction

Florida. The Sunshine State.

Is it a land of natural beauty, or a land of dreaded change?

In our opinion it remains a bit of the first, and a lot of the second. Florida has changed dramatically in physical appearance and demographics over a period of only fifty years.

The changes are nowhere more apparent than to naturalists. Florida's great lake, Lake Okeechobee, has been diked and tamed, vast expanses of the Everglades have been drained, and where sawgrass once bowed before subtropical breezes, sugarcane and sod fields now reign supreme. Miami—only 50 years ago a small, friendly town with open windows, doors, and hearts—is now an impersonal, at times seemingly hostile—megalopolis.

Although changes similar to those in Miami have occurred up and down the peninsula and westward on the panhandle, there are still large areas of "natural Florida" left. Whether they are left to be preserved or left to be plundered is still to be determined.

In the reduced and still diminishing bit of natural Florida, 68 species and subspecies of amphibians can be found. This number is almost evenly divided between the anurans (the tail-less frogs, toads, and treefrogs) and the caudatans (the salamanders and, if we wish to differentiate them a bit, the newts).

Many of the amphibians are wide ranging and common. Among these are the southern toad, the green treefrog, the introduced Cuban treefrog, and the greater siren. Some, such as the Pine Barrens treefrog, the striped newt, and the two species of flatwoods salamanders, are very much reduced in numbers, and concern is now being voiced about the possibility of their extinction.

1

Sixty-three species of Florida's amphibian fauna are native. The five introduced species are as follows:

Cane toad: firmly established
Cuban treefrog: firmly established
Greenhouse frog: firmly established
Puerto Rican coqui: tenuous
Australian great green treefrog: status unknown.

Many of our native amphibian species are crowded out in areas of urban and suburban sprawl, but at least four of the five alien forms not only easily survive the changes wrought by man but are most common in the proximity of human-altered habitats as well (the habitat parameters required by the Australian great green treefrog have not yet been defined in Florida).

How stable are populations of Florida's amphibians? Opinions vary widely. If for no other reason than the fact that commercial collecting of native amphibians from the wild continues to be allowed, a conservationist could surmise from the stance of the state's Fish and Wildlife Conservation Commission that most amphibians continue to do well. This may or may not actually be the case. As an example, although they seem common in other areas, river frogs were hard to find in northeastern Florida in 2008 and 2009. Why? It just may be that the regulatory arm of the commission is moving a little more slowly than many of us would like to protect our native amphibians from overexploitation. Currently the commission offers some measure of protection to only 6 of our 68 species and subspecies of amphibians. No exotics are protected.

Biologists from other agencies and myriad independent biologists and researchers feel that more protection should be offered to more species, and that the Fish and Wildlife Conservation Commission should provide that protection now—a situation probably quite typical of conservationists and official bureaucracies in all states.

Despite increasing tolerance of amphibians (and even of reptiles), there remain many pressures on Florida's herpetofauna. Among others are the following:

• continued habitat degradation
• carnage on canal-side, pond side, and other highways
• nonregulated collecting for the pet trade

- nonregulated collecting for scientific research
- increased presence of pathogens

Ensuring that all the amphibians (and reptiles) of Florida are here for us and our descendants to view and appreciate in the wild will take a concerted effort on the part of all persons. Whether we are researchers, herpetoculturists, or merely people with an interest in the creatures with which we share our world, it is time for us to join forces and promote the conservation of these interesting, beneficial, and highly evolved animals. We hope that our comments in this identification guide will help you better understand and appreciate the intricate lifestyles of Florida's amphibians. As is so often said, "we're all in this together," so let's all work together.

# Amphibians Defined

The ancestors of today's amphibians evolved from the fishes some 350 million years ago, during the early Devonian period.

Today, the class Amphibia contains three groups comprising rather divergent-appearing creatures.

These groups include the frogs (including toads and treefrogs), the salamanders, and the caecilians, totaling about 4,000 species. Representatives of only the first two groups occur in Florida.

Though of diverse appearance, amphibians have many characteristics in common. They have moist skins that lack such cover as hair, feathers, and scales; they lack true claws; and by definition (but sometimes not in actuality) amphibians lead a double life.

The double life about which we speak is rather a normality for amphibians, though. Many breed and lay their eggs in the water. Those eggs hatch into aquatic larvae that develop and eventually reach a point of metamorphosis. During metamorphosis, changes occur, including resorption of gills, development of eyelids, and skin cell changes, and the aquatic larvae leave the water to begin life on land. However, at no point in its life is any amphibian truly divorced from an external source of moisture. Even in species adapted to aridland habitats, life-enabling moisture must be absorbed through the skin.

There are, of course, divergences, or seeming divergences from the norm. Some amphibians are fully aquatic throughout their lives. Others are not dependent on the availability of free-standing water and live a fully terrestrial existence. But all amphibians—there are *no* exceptions— must at some time nearly every day be in contact with some source of external moisture.

A few amphibians give birth to living young; however, most, including all Florida species, reproduce by means of gelatinous-covered eggs.

The eggs are laid in the water or in moisture-retaining terrestrial situations, often very near water.

Amphibians lack scales and claws and usually have a moist skin (the skin of toads and some newts is warty and rather dry). Florida examples include frogs, toads, treefrogs (all typified by muscular hind legs used for jumping or hopping) and salamanders, including newts (which are elongate, some superficially lizardlike, and have two or four tiny to moderate legs of about the same size).

The families appear as follows in accounts 1–71:

Frogs, Toads, and Treefrogs 1–36 & 69
    Bufonidae: Toads 1–4
    Eleutherodactylidae: Tropical Frogs 5–6
    Hylidae: Treefrogs and Allies 7–25
    Microhylidae: Narrow-mouthed Toads 26
    Ranidae: True Frogs 27–35 & 69
    Scaphiopodidae: Spadefoot Toads 36
Salamanders 37–68 & 70–71
    Ambystomatidae: Mole Salamanders 37–41 & 70
    Amphiumidae: Amphiumas 42–43 & 71
    Plethodontidae: Lungless Salamanders 44–57
    Proteidae: Waterdogs 58
    Salamandridae: Newts 59–61
    Sirenidae: Sirens 62–68

# How to Use This Book

In these pages we discuss 71 species and subspecies of amphibians, 68 of which occur in Florida and 3 peripheral species. Many are of very dissimilar appearance, but some are confusingly alike.

We have opted to list and discuss all in a traditional manner, divided by families, genera, species, and subspecies.

We have also opted, for the most part, to use well-established, standardized common and scientific names. Future changes in both will probably occur.

We have listed and numbered all species and subspecies in the table of contents. Those numbers coincide with the numbers mentioned in both text and photographs. If you know, or have a good idea of, the name of the species you are researching, begin with the table of contents.

We have listed each major group, genus, species, and subspecies alphabetically by scientific name; therefore, you may have to search a while if you know only the common name of a species, and check the photo and range map provided for each species.

Scientific names are of Latin or Greek derivation. They can be binomial (two names) or trinomial (three names).

Examples of each are as follows:

Southern toad, *Bufo terrestris* (pronounced boo-fo terr-ess-tris). This common toad, found from backyard to wilderness areas, has not subspeciated; thus it is identified by only a binomial.

Western bird-voiced treefrog, *Hyla avivoca avivoca* (pronounced hi-laa av-ee-vo-kaw). The trinomial indicates that this small frog is subspeciated. The redundant specific and subspecific names indicate that this subspecies is the nominate race (the first subspecies identified). There is only one other race of *Hyla avivoca*, the eastern bird-voiced treefrog (*Hyla avivoca ogechiensis*). It does not occur in Florida.

If you are able to place an amphibian in a family or group (a toad, a frog, a treefrog, or a salamander, or even more generally just as a frog or a salamander), it will speed the process of identification.

Since they are readily recognized by most persons, let's use a garden-variety "hop-toad" found in the western panhandle as an example:

First, this toad, like all toads of the United States, has a dryish, warty skin, muscular hind legs, and no scales or claws. This combination of characteristics tells us it is both an amphibian and a toad. You will quickly see that there are only four toad species in Florida, and a glance at the range maps shows that of the four, only three occur on Florida's panhandle.

Your toad is about 2 inches long. If you compare the specimen at hand with the photos of the three possible species, you may be able to make an immediate identification. But if identification by photo is not possible, move on to the species accounts. According to the accounts, one of the possible species, the oak toad, is only about an inch in length when full grown. By discounting it you have narrowed your search to either the southern or the Fowler's toad.

The accounts then tell you that the southern toad has knobby protuberances on the back of its head and may be dark spotted, and, if spots are present, they usually enclose only one but sometimes two or more warts.

Your specimen has no conspicuous knobs on its head, and it has prominent light-edged dark spots, most of which contain three or more warts. An additional (but not infallible) clue to the identities of toads is color. In the Florida panhandle, southern toads are often quite red in color. Fowler's toads are almost always grayish; thus you discount the southern toad and are left, through elimination (a nonscientific but often effective method of arriving at an answer), with the Fowler's toad. Check the photo again and you will probably now see the resemblance.

# Key to Families of Florida Amphibians

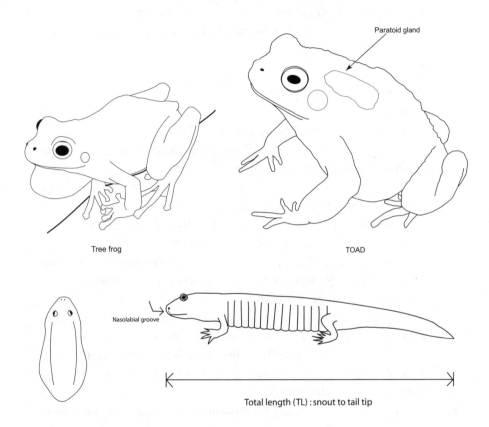

Paratoid gland

Tree frog

TOAD

Nasolabial groove

Total length (TL) : snout to tail tip

## Anurans

1. Skin warty, tuberculate, or nearly smooth; build "pudgy" . . . . . . . . 2
   Skin nearly smooth or ridged dorsolaterally . . . . . . . . . . . . . . . . . . . 3
2. Skin warty, parotoid (shoulder) glands distinct, pupils horizontal . .
   . . . . . . . . . . . . . . . . . . . . . . . . . . . . . **Family Bufonidae, Toads**
   Skin nearly smooth, parotoid glands indistinct, pupils vertical . . . . .
   . . . . . . . . . . . . . . . . . . . . . . **Family Scaphiopodidae, Spadefoots**

3. Toes fully or almost fully webbed . . . . . . . . . . . . . . . . . . . . . . . . . . . . . 4
   Toes unwebbed. . . . . . . . . . . . . . . . . . . . . . . . . . . . . . . . . . . . . . . . . . . . . 5
4. Size large (greater than 1 inch). . . . . . . . **Family Ranidae, True Frogs**
   Size small (under 1 inch). . . . . . . . . . . . . . . . . . . . . . . . . . . . . . . . . . . . .
   . . . . . . . . . . . . . . . . . . . . . **Family Hylidae (in part), Cricket Frogs**
5. Size tiny, head broad, snout rather bluntly rounded. . . . . . . . . . . . . . .
   . . . . . . . . . . . . . . . . . . . . . **Family Leptodactylidae, Tropical Frogs**
   Size tiny, fold of skin at back of head, snout pointed . . . . . . . . . . . . .
   . . . . . . . . . . . . . . . **Family Microhylidae, Narrow-mouthed Toads**

## Caudatans

1. Body elongate, eel-like, aquatic . . . . . . . . . . . . . . . . . . . . . . . . . . . . . . . 2
   Body otherwise . . . . . . . . . . . . . . . . . . . . . . . . . . . . . . . . . . . . . . . . . . . . 3
2. Two pairs of very tiny legs, no external gills . . . . . . . . . . . . . . . . . . . .
   . . . . . . . . . . . . . . . . . . . . . . . . . **Family Amphiumidae, Amphiumas**
   Forelimbs only, 3 pairs of bushy external gills. . . . . . . . . . . . . . . . . . .
   . . . . . . . . . . . . . . . . . . . . . . . . . . . . . . . . . **Family Sirenidae, Sirens**
3. Costal grooves present . . . . . . . . . . . . . . . . . . . . . . . . . . . . . . . . . . . . . 4
   Costal grooves absent . . . . . . . . . . . . **Family Salamandridae, Newts**
4. Four toes on all feet, 3 pairs of bushy external gills present at all
   life stages, aquatic . . . . . . . . . . . . . . . . **Family Proteidae, Waterdogs**
   Usually 5 (rarely 4) toes on rear feet, adults of most species
   normally without external gills (see exceptions noted in
   family Plethodontidae). . . . . . . . . . . . . . . . . . . . . . . . . . . . . . . . . . . . 5
5. Two pairs of legs, 5 toes on rear feet, nasolabial grooves absent. . . . .
   . . . . . . . . . . . . . . . . . **Family Ambystomatidae, Mole Salamanders**
   Nasolabial grooves present (see note below for additional
   identifying characteristics). . . . . . . . . . . . . . . . . . . . . . . . . . . . . . . . . .
   . . . . . . . . . . . . . . . **Family Plethodontidae, Lungless Salamanders**

Note: Florida salamanders of the family Plethodontidae have two pairs of legs, 5 toes on rear feet (except for *Hemidactylium scutatum* and *Eurycea quadridigitata*, which have 4 toes on all feet), bushy external gills present only in larval stages (except for the cave-dwelling, aquatic, pigmentless *Eurycea wallacei*, which has gills but lacks functional eyes throughout life).

# Florida's Habitats

To find a particular species or subspecies of amphibian in Florida, you must look first within its range and next in proper habitat.

Amphibians may actually be restricted to a very specific habitat (and perhaps their immediate surroundings), or they may be able to utilize a wider spectrum of habitats. For example, while the eastern Gulf Coast waterdog is able to exist only in a few streams in Florida's panhandle, the southern toad may be encountered statewide in urban backyards, remote forestlands, and coastal strands.

## Xeric (dry) Uplands—standing water is uncommon

1. Scrub: Sandy, rapidly drained soils typify this habitat as does a plant community of sand pine, *Opuntia* cactus, rosemary, wiregrass, and lichens.

    Amphibians such as the oak toad, gopher frog, and spadefoot occur in this habitat.

2. Sandhills: Soils are sandy and fast draining. The typical plant community consists of turkey oak, longleaf pine, wiregrasses, and saw palmetto.

This habitat supports such amphibian species as the gopher frog, spadefoot, and slimy salamander.

3. Hammocks (oak, etc.): Red, bluejack, live, and laurel oaks are typical trees replacing the pines in these successional areas, but poor soils restrict succession to true woodlands. Wire and other grasses are present. Shallow, ephemeral ponds may be present.

This habitat supports such amphibian species as the gopher frog, spadefoot, tiger salamander, and flatwoods salamander.

## Mesic (damp) Uplands—ephemeral or permanent ponds or streams may be present.

4. Hardwoods: An overstory community of oaks, beeches, magnolias, and other tall forest trees is present. Understory trees and shrubs, such as American holly and hophornbean, are present. Catsclaw, grape, ferns, and other vines and forest floor plants are usually evident.

   This habitat supports such amphibian species as the dwarf salamander, two-lined salamander, mole salamander, and gray treefrog.

5. Pine: Longleaf pines are the dominant overstory tree in this community. A shrubby understory may or may not be present, but grasses and herbaceous growth grow thickly on the forest floor.

Oak toads, spadefoots, and two-lined salamanders call this habitat home.

## Mesic (damp) Flatlands—ephemeral or permanent ponds may be present.

6. Pine Flatwoods: With stands of natural or cultured longleaf pine as the dominant overstory tree, pine flatwoods are typified by poorly drained soils, a sparse understory at best, but profuse ground cover.

   Look for species such as the flatwoods salamander, slimy salamander, ornate chorus frog, oak toad, and pine woods treefrog here.

7. Prairie: A dense growth of herbaceous ground cover typifies this open, usually treeless habitat. Such understory plants as saw palmetto and willows may be abundant, especially around waterholes and canals.

   Seek peninsula newts as well as pig frogs and leopard frogs at waterholes.

## Hydric Flatlands—flatlands subject to periodic flooding

8. Wet Marl Prairies: These poorly drained prairies are most common on the southern peninsula. They are open, treeless expanses that may support some stands of shrubs and a dense ground cover of wiregrass, rushes, spider lilies, and other flood-tolerant plants.

Amphibians such as the pig frog and leopard frog may be found here.

9. River Swamps: Sweet gum, bay, and maples are among the more commonly seen larger trees in this habitat. Both species of titi, wax myrtle, and other shrubs and myriad low-light, ground-dwelling herbs occur on the forest floor.

Expect to find the gray treefrog, green treefrog, bird-voiced treefrog, mole salamander, and southern dusky salamander in this habitat.

10. Cypress Swamps and Heads: This habitat is flooded for much, if not all, of each year. Besides cypress, trees such as sweet gum and elder grow. Where conditions permit, shrubs and emergent herbs occur.

Three-lined salamander, two-toed amphiuma, bullfrog, pig frog, and river frog may be encountered in this habitat.

11. Everglades Hammocks/Swales: At one time this habitat, with its shallow, flowing waters, was found over much of the southern peninsula of Florida. Today it is restricted to outflows from Lake Okeechobee and the Big Cypress regions. Sawgrass and other plants that thrive with perpetually wet feet are typical of this habitat.

The two-toed amphiuma, greater siren, pig frog, bronze frog, and southern leopard frog occur in these swales.

## Limestone Communities—canals have been dug through many of these habitats.

12. Pine Rocklands: Restricted to the southern peninsula and the Keys, this habitat supports sparse to moderate stands of slash pines beneath which grows a ground cover of drought tolerant ferns, terrestrial orchids, cat-briar, and harsh grasses.

    The greenhouse frog, narrow-mouthed toad, and Cuban treefrog reside in this type of habitat.

13. Limestone Hardwood Hammock: Restricted to the southernmost areas of the state, these are elevated hammocks of densely growing tropical and temperate tree species such as live oaks, gumbo-limbo, poisonwood, tamarind, and *Paurotis* and *Sabal* palms.

The Cuban treefrog, squirrel treefrog, greenhouse frog, and giant toad frequent these hammocks.

## Disturbed Habitats

14. Human habitations (including buildings, yards, urban parklands, roadside trash piles and recreational areas).

    The Puerto Rican coqui, greenhouse frog, and narrow-mouthed toad are abundant within their respective ranges.

15. Modified habitats (pastures, fields, farmlands, agricultural areas). Look for the oak toad, southern toad, green treefrog, squirrel treefrog, and leopard frog in this habitat.

## Freshwater and Marine Habitats

16. Shady creeks, streams, and their adjacent mucklands and sphagnum bogs.

     Aquatic species such as waterdogs and dusky salamanders may be found in the creeks, and red salamanders, mud salamanders, and one-toed amphiuma in the muck beds. Four-toed salamanders, bog frogs, carpenter frogs, and Apalachicola dusky salamanders inhabit the sphagnaceous areas.

17. Ephemeral ponds and flooded ditches: These are poorly drained, low-lying (often manmade) areas that fill regularly during the rainy seasons but dry regularly between heavy rains. Drought-tolerant aquatic vegetation and immersion-tolerant semiterrestrial plants usually abound in these habitats.

    Many treefrogs, toads, and narrow-mouthed toads are commonly found here.

18. Permanent ponds, lakes, and canals: Although water levels may fluctuate with rainfall, permanent ponds, lakes, and canals usually retain water year-round. Shrubs often rim the perimeters, and emergent vegetation may grow thickly in the shallows. Submerged vegetation of many kinds grow where the water becomes too deep for emergents.

Frogs, toads, treefrogs, and amphiuma as well as greater and lesser sirens may be encountered in this habitat.

19. Freshwater marshes: These are low-lying, poorly drained habitats that usually hold water. Cattail, pickerelweed, alligator flag, blue flag, and maidencane are commonly seen emergents, and shrubs such as wax myrtle and various willows often surround the area.

    Look for the aquatic salamanders and many true frogs in this habitat.

20. Steepheads: These are acidic boggy hillside seepages created by water percolating through porous deep sandy soils until diverted by clay subsoil. Insectivorous plants, grasses, and dense herbaceous growth typify these habitats.

    Pine Barrens treefrogs, green treefrogs, cricket frogs, two-lined salamanders, and dusky salamanders may be found in this habitat.

Photo by Carl D. May

21. Streams, creeks, and rivers: These may fluctuate in depth but are typified by flowing water throughout the year. Generally speaking, rivers are larger than creeks and streams. Many originate from freshwater springheads in densely wooded areas but meander near their mouths through tidal marshlands or mangrove swamps. Depending on water depth and soil conditions, both emergent and submerged vegetation may be abundant.

Terrestrial salamanders such as two-lined, three-lined, and duskies dwell on the banks, while two-toed amphiuma, greater sirens, and lesser sirens and the larvae of many other species occur in aquatic situations.

22. Coastal dunes and high beaches: These are above the high water mark in all but the most severe conditions. Sea oats, beach morning glory, saw palmetto, and other shrubs are typical plants.

   This is a poor area for amphibians, but occasionally spadefoots and southern toads may be found here.

23. Mangrove swamps: These are low-lying, tidally influenced zones of transition between fresh and salt waters vegetated by red, black, and white mangroves and buttonwood.

Leopard frogs and green treefrogs may occur in this habitat.

24. Saltmarsh: These are heavily vegetated, open regions of tidally influenced shoreline. The salinity is very variable. Cord and salt grasses and rushes are usually the dominant plants.

Few amphibians occur regularly in this habitat. Occasionally leopard frogs and green treefrogs may inhabit areas of weak salinity.

25. Open ocean (including shorelines and estuaries).
No amphibians occur here.

# Amphibians as Captives

## Laws and Regulations

A word of caution: before collecting or molesting amphibians in the wild, we urge you to check the list of protected or regulated species below. In some instances, it is perfectly legal for you to collect a specimen (sometimes two) of state-regulated species, but you need to know what is legal and what is not. Check with the regulatory division of Florida's Fish and Wildlife Conservation Commission for particulars. Violating the laws protecting reptiles and amphibians is a serious offense. Don't become an arrest statistic.

Protected or regulated species in Florida in 2009:

*Ambystoma bishopi*, reticulated flatwoods salamander
*Ambystoma cingulatum*, frosted flatwoods salamander
*Eurycea* (*Haideotriton*) *wallacei*, Georgia blind salamander
*Hyla andersonii*, Pine Barrens treefrog
*Rana capito*, gopher frog
*Rana okaloosae*, Florida bog frog

These amphibians should not be molested or collected without a permit. Bag limits may be set for other amphibian species.

Keep in mind the term "molest" can be broadly interpreted by law enforcement personnel. Ostensibly, it can include even photographing in the wild if the progress of an animal is interrupted or if it is startled into motion. Because laws and regulations are subject to change, we suggest you contact the appropriate regulatory agency for current listings and interpretations.

## Care of Captive Amphibians

Keeping amphibians in captivity is a popular and still-growing hobby. A vast amount of money is spent annually in the acquisition of amphibians and support equipment such as cages, cage furniture, food items, etc.

Many of Florida's amphibians figure prominently in the pet trade. Among these are species such as marbled and tiger salamanders, greater and lesser sirens, two-toed amphiuma, barking, green, and Cuban treefrogs, southern toads, and bullfrogs. Very few of these are captive bred. Another way of saying this is to simply state that nearly all of these offered in the pet trade are collected from the wild. Some people eke out a marginal living by collecting amphibians from the wild to sell to wholesalers.

Despite ready availability of wild-collected amphibians, we advocate the purchase of domestically bred specimens whenever possible.

The long-term maintenance of amphibians is not always as simple as it would initially seem. Certainly merely putting the specimen in question in a suitably sized terrarium and providing food and water will suffice for the short term, but for the long term, many species need more. To be a truly successful herpetoculturist, learning the life history of your charges—especially their behaviors, microhabitat, and food requirements—is an absolute must. Here are a few generalized examples:

Terrestrial salamanders, frogs, toads, and treefrogs absorb their water needs through their skin. They dwell in moist (but often not wet) surroundings and do not need a dish of water.

Waterdogs and many-lined salamanders are fully aquatic. They thrive best in chlorine/chloramine-free water of a pH similar (or at least close) to that in which they occur in the wild.

Dusky salamanders, red salamanders, and brook salamanders like wet (simulated stream-edge) situations.

Woodland salamanders, mole salamanders, and four-toed salamanders like damp, not wet situations.

Some frogs—leopard frogs, bullfrogs, and bronze frogs among them—thermoregulate by sitting or floating in the sunlight.

Some "treefrogs" prefer grasses or emergent vegetation over trees.

Terrestrial salamanders require a nonabrasive burrowing medium and an equally nonirritating surface cover beneath which they can reside when not actually burrowed.

Aquatic salamanders (including larval salamanders of many terrestrial forms) and tadpoles need chlorine/chloramine-free water of a pH similar (or at least close) to that in which they occur in the wild.

Calcium: Some amphibians, ranid frogs among them, may bask in full spectrum lighting to produce and metabolize calcium, but since many amphibians are creatures of the shade, darkness, and burrows, it is thought that sunlight (most especially the ultraviolet spectra, UV-A and UV-B) plays a lesser role with the nonbasking forms.

For these latter it would seem that the only valid method of providing dietary calcium augmentation to captives would be through use of calcium as a food supplement. This can be accomplished by injecting a food item with a minuscule droplet of liquid calcium, by coating feed insects with a fine powdered D3-calcium mixture, or by "gut-loading" feed insects. But provide calcium with reasonable care, keeping in mind all the while that adult amphibians require less calcium than rapidly growing babies. Too much calcium can actually be harmful, for it can be drawn into the viscera, creating lesions and gout.

Our recommendation is, whenever possible, go natural. Provide unfiltered sunlight or use full spectrum bulbs for those basking species that will use it, and allow your specimens to synthesize and metabolize their calcium needs in a wholly natural manner. When this is not possible, provide additives, but do so sparingly, and use mixtures that contain at least twice as much calcium as phosphorus.

At this moment we are much less certain of the nutritional and housing needs of amphibians than of reptiles. But we're learning.

The terrarium: Provide a terrarium with enough space for your amphibian pets. Research the basic needs of the species with which you're working, then improve those basics by at least 25%.

Terraria may be built in a number of formats, woodland, sand ridge-savanna, semiaquatic, and aquatic among them. Terraria may be horizontally oriented for terrestrial species or vertically oriented for arboreal species. In general, amphibians will not need an additional heat source nor are they apt to use thermal gradients.

There are now many types of commercially available cages. Choose one spacious enough for the amphibian you wish to keep. All terraria should have escape-proof covers. A cover is not a luxury; it is a necessity.

It is important that all captive anurans feel secure in their cages. If they do not, they may persistently jump against the sides or top, eventually breaking the skin on their nose or chin and injuring their legs. Visual barriers such as plants or clean soil into which the frogs may burrow can provide the needed security. Treefrogs should be provided with well-anchored branches or plants on which they can climb.

Since amphibians have delicate, permeable skin through which both moisture and accumulated impurities are absorbed, absolute cage cleanliness is a necessity. Handle all amphibians carefully and only when necessary.

Despite being creatures of the soil, leaf litter, and aquatic habitats, salamanders and newts can and will climb to escape. Keep their terrarium tightly covered.

Aquatic species such as sirens, amphiuma, waterdogs, and tadpoles can be kept in a setup such as you would provide for fish. The larger aquatic salamanders will often uproot aquatic plants. Adequate filtration and water quality (pH, dH, ammonia levels, etc.) are necessary to successfully keep aquatic amphibians. Research your captive well.

Aquatic salamanders are very adept at escaping through openings around filters and related objects. They use the moisture in their skin to help them climb nonporous surfaces. Close all openings.

Above all, if you lose interest in your amphibian, either find it a new home with an enthusiastic keeper or return it to the breeders. Do not release it into the wild, even if it is a native species (and releasing a non-native species is unthinkable). Releasing a creature into an area where it has no established home range places it at an enormous disadvantage.

## Diet

Frogs, Toads and Treefrogs, Salamanders and Newts: Smaller types of frogs, toads, and treefrogs are all insectivorous; the larger ones vary an insect diet with small fish, crayfish, other frogs, and even an occasional small rodent. Some, such as the little grass frog and the narrow-mouthed toad, require a diet of termite- or fruit fly–sized insects. Slightly larger ones such as oak toads, chorus, and cricket frogs will eat insects up to the size of one-quarter of a grown cricket. Treefrogs will often accept proportionately larger prey than other amphibian species. An inch-long squirrel treefrog, for instance, will eat a half-grown cricket. Adult anurans the size of fully grown green and gray treefrogs, southern toads, or leopard frogs (this means a body length of 3–4 inches) will readily consume fully grown crickets. Pig frogs and bullfrogs will vary an insect diet by eating smaller frogs and an occasional baby mouse ("occasional" means just that; high-fat items like mice contribute to lipid buildups in the eyes, which can result in blindness). Earthworms or nightcrawlers are fine foods for all anurans.

Mole salamanders are also partial to worms, often accepting these even if refusing all else. Adult tiger salamanders are large enough to accept an occasional newly born mouse. Baby crickets, fruit flies, termites, and springtails are accepted by most of the smaller species of salamanders and newts. Tedious though this method may be, we have fed and kept some salamanders for long periods by offering earthworm sections impaled on a broomstraw and gently waved in front of them (this works for small frogs, too).

"Gut-load" the insects you offer your amphibians by feeding the insects well. Dust the insects with a D3-calcium based vitamin powder before feeding them to your reptiles and amphibians, but some hobbyists feel the self-cleaning nature of crickets means they'll divest themselves of their "vitamin jackets" within an hour or two.

# Digital Photography

## Field and Stage

Photographing amphibians in the field or in a staged set-up can change your perspective of what's beautiful. A close-up shot of the head of a red salamander, or an overview of a pine barrens treefrog has a tendency to make one stop and muse, "y'know, that's really . . . pretty!" and soon you have 18 x 24-inch color prints of different kinds of amphibians on every wall of your house. Looking around our own home, we think there's absolutely nothing wrong with this.

In a purely practical sense, photography can be the least obtrusive way to document captive or wild behavior patterns, especially with the convenience of digital photography. The instant feedback of digital photography has taken a lot of the mystery out of getting a good shot. (In lieu of a preserved voucher specimen, a high-quality photo may be acceptable to museums for documenting the presence of a given species—but a museum is going to want the preserved animal nonetheless.)

Taking a good photograph of an amphibian in the field requires knowledge of how soon that amphibian will react to the presence of a human as well as a bit of stealth, and a working knowledge of photography. Getting started is easy . . .

The equipment required depends on a number of variables. Whether you're photographing long-distance habitat shots, taking close-ups in the field, or placing the snake on a stage are all factors to consider.

Photographing an amphibian under controlled, staged conditions is infinitely easier than taking photos in the field, but figuring out how to position it—or waiting until the creature positions itself—is still time-consuming.

## Basic Equipment Needs

A sturdy digital camera body with interchangeable lenses (single lens reflex [SLR] capabilities) is suggested, but with today's technology, not an absolute necessity. You may be able to get the results you want with a simple (that term is subjective) digital camera without interchangeable lenses, called a point and shoot camera, and such a camera is much easier to carry and set up. Check the Web for up-to-date information on options you want—we like the LCD that can tilt so you can see what you're photographing even if the camera is flat on the ground, and 7 megapixels is sufficient capacity for details. If you need some quick help in assessing features in a digital camera, two helpful on-line sites are http://www.pcworld.com/article/125645/how_to_buy_a_digital_camera.html and http://solution.allthingsd.com/20070509/how-to-buy-your-next-digital-camera/

At one time, we would have suggested considering good quality secondhand equipment, but new digital equipment is much more affordable than the old film cameras. You should join a list-serve of photo hobbyists who share their experiences with various brands and models, because there's a lot to choose from. Most of us buy our equipment from discount electronics stores, so impartial advice is important. If you have access to a photo supply dealer who can accurately advise you about the condition of the equipment you're buying, and who can tell you about some features of that particular lens or body, treasure this person and buy from him or her.

Suggested Lenses

> 28 mm wide angle for habitat photos
> 50 mm standard for habitat photos
> 100 mm macro for close-ups (suitable for almost every purpose)
> 75–205 mm zoom lens for variable field work
> 300 or 400 mm fixed focal length telephoto lens for field work (the 300 is by far the easiest to hand-hold)

Or a point and shoot camera with both close-up capabilities and a high quality 10X, 12X, or 20X zoom lens affixed.

## Flash units

One or more dedicated flash units (a dedicated flash interfaces with the camera's f-stop setting to furnish appropriate light levels). Teleconverters in strengths of 1.25 to 2.0.

## Flashlight

A flashlight is a necessity for nighttime photography. We affix a small flashlight to the top of our flash unit with short strips of Velcro. Our flashlight operates on two AA batteries. This self-contained arrangement allows a single person to focus on subjects at night in the field.

## Tripod

Although a sturdy tripod was once an absolute necessity for holding the larger magnification telephoto lenses steady, some of today's better cameras have an antishake or stabilization factor built in. A steady camera ensures no blurring when you squeeze that "once in a lifetime" shot. With a tripod, a cable release ensures additional stability.

If ever your camera will malfunction, it will be at a critical time, when you are faced with an opportunity to take a "once in a lifetime" shot. It is always a good idea to have at least one spare camera body available.

## Some Photography Hints

For staged photography, create a small natural setting by placing rocks, mosses, leaves, or bark—whatever is most appropriate for the species you're photographing—on a stage. A stage can be as simple as an old cardboard box or a large lazy susan draped in black velvet, or as sophisticated as you choose to make it. If you don't have a lazy susan or similar contained area, just arrange the setting on a table top or a tree stump, wherever you are at the time. Ideally, once you have constructed your background, you will merely put the specimen in place, focus, and shoot; however, seldom are things ideal. Many herps are nervous, and it will take dedication, gentleness, and patience on your part to accomplish your goal. Having a photo assistant to help pose or repose, or to catch and recatch the subject will help. Move slowly at all times when working with any amphibian or reptile.

Our stage for contrived shots is easily movable and always in the back of the car when we travel. It consists of the top half of a round trash can bolted to a large lazy susan. Black velvet clipped around the inside surface of the background gives a good unobtrusive background for our photographic efforts. We use one or more add-on flash units when light levels are low.

Again, remember to move very slowly when approaching an amphibian in the field. Approach it slowly and obliquely. Avoid eye contact. If the amphibian notices you (as it almost certainly will), freeze for a moment until it relaxes, then resume the stalk. You may eventually get close enough to make the field shot for which you were hoping. When shooting in the field, retrace your steps carefully, disturbing as little habitat as possible and leaving nothing behind—nothing, that is, but your footprints and the specimen you just successfully photographed.

What about biting insects? Inure yourself. They'll be there. Field photography means contending with biting flies by day, mosquitoes and no-see-ums by night, and ticks and chiggers at both times. You can spare yourself a lot of grief by wearing socks, long pants, a long-sleeved shirt with a collar you can turn up, and a hat with a floppy brim. You can spray your cuffs, collar, and hat brim with insect repellent to keep your hands clean. If you must use insect repellent on your skin, apply it before you need it and wash your hands carefully after applying. Do not get any topical insecticide or repellent on your camera equipment. In addition to wreaking havoc on camera equipment, topical insecticides left on your hands can be instantly fatal to any amphibian or reptile you touch.

# Toxicity and Other Potential Problems

Although it only makes sense to wash your hands after handling an amphibian or reptile, we felt a word of caution about possible toxicity and other potential dangers of a few species is needed.

All amphibians exude skin secretions that may retard desiccation or afford protection from predators. Newts, cane toads, pickerel frogs, and Cuban treefrogs are all known to produce particularly virulent exudates. These exudates are especially effective when ingested or brought into contact with mucous membranes (nose, mouth, eyes) or open wounds. One of us essentially wept during the entire drive from Miami to Ft. Myers after handling a Cuban Tree frog and forgetting the hand-washing rule.

Keep in mind that your hands are hot, about 95 °F or so. An amphibian with surface temp a cool 65 °F may find your touch uncomfortable. Don't hold any amphibian longer than absolutely necessary.

# Taxonomy

The science of classification is called taxonomy. With the changing times have come often-conflicting methods of determining the long-time standing and validity of amphibian families, genera, species, and, especially, subspecies.

The traditional method of species determination was known as Linnaean taxonomy (biological classification). In this method the validity of a species was determined largely by its similarities to or differences from other taxa. Visible physical (structural) similarities and an ability to interbreed and produce viable young were important criteria. Subspecies were recognized on what was loosely termed the "75% rule": if 75% of a given population was different from the next in some recognizable manner, for example, color, pattern, or scalation, but still able to interbreed, the population satisfied the criterion of subspecies. As an example, the Linnaean system of taxonomy recognized the northern cricket frog, *Acris crepitans crepitans*, and two additional subspecies, the pinkish-bellied coastal cricket frog, *A. c. paludicola*, and the widespread Blanchard's cricket frog, *A. c. blanchardi*.

Although the Linnaean system of taxonomy was inexact, the trinomial nomenclature bestowed on the cricket frogs indicates a rather consistent difference in appearance between the three cricket frog subspecies but also that they are related, and that they can (and do) interbreed and produce viable offspring.

The Linnaean system is still widely accepted, but it is now being challenged by phylogenetic (evolutionary) philosophies. The role of molecular data in species determination has already undergone several metamorphoses and will probably undergo several more before becoming universal in use. Many hope a system of logical checks and balances, now sadly missing, will be among the improvements.

Mitochondrial DNA (mtDNA) was among the first of the molecular technologies used. Although it is still used in some analyses, it was quickly learned that because mtDNA is passed on matrilineally, even the most tedious analysis garnered only part of the answer. A better tool is the use of nuclear DNA (nDNA), which is passed on sexually and provides more substantive data.

Because traditional systematics uses physical characteristics and because we feel that a field guide is not the proper forum for arguing taxonomic principles, we have retained this comfortable and conservative approach.

Wherever we felt them suitable, both the common and scientific names used in this book are those suggested in the publication titled *Scientific and Standard English Names of Amphibians and Reptiles of North America North of Mexico, with Comments Regarding Confidence in our Understanding*. This effort at standardization of names incorporated the opinions of many herpetologists and was compiled and edited for SSAR by Brian I. Crother of Southeastern Louisiana University in Hammond.

Listed below are just a few proposed changes that are still controversial. Other, less sweeping, proposed changes are mentioned in individual species accounts.

| Proposed name | Current name | For |
| --- | --- | --- |
| Lithobates | Rana | Ranid frogs of the eastern United States |
| Anaxyrus | Bufo | Most North American toads |
| *Rhinella* | *Bufo* | Cane toad |

# Frogs, Toads, and Treefrogs (Anura)

Not all frogs are toads, nor are all frogs treefrogs, but all toads and tree-frogs are frogs.

This is just another way of saying that the toads and the treefrogs are simply frogs that have developed a certain set of characteristics that allow observers and systematists to conveniently group them together.

Representatives of six families of anurans are found in Florida.

No matter the family to which they belong, the frogs, toads, and tree-frogs of Florida have lidded eyes, moist skins (sometimes difficult to determine on dusty toads), and muscular hind legs for hopping or leaping. The males (and sometimes the females) of all have one or more rather distinctive calls.

All except the two species of greenhouse frogs have an aquatic larval (tadpole) stage, and all are terrestrial or semiaquatic as adults. The two greenhouse frogs lay their eggs in moist pockets on land and full development occurs in the egg capsule.

## How to Find Frogs, Toads, and Treefrogs in Florida

In nearly every case, frogs, toads, and treefrogs are most easily found at night by using a flashlight, when they are vocalizing at breeding ponds. They are most difficult to find at midday in midsummer or during very cold, dry winter weather.

Additionally, amphibians are most easily approached for observation (including photographing) on fairly warm overcast or misty nights. They are especially approachable when these nights occur in conjunction with lowered barometric pressure. All can be very difficult to approach on brilliantly moonlit night. If you are wading into water to find them, do so slowly and without creating ripples.

Frogs, toads, and treefrogs are found throughout the state of Florida. All species and subspecies, except the two species of tropical frogs, may be found at breeding ponds at some time of the year. They may be tracked, and are identifiable, by their voices. The two tropical frogs also call, but from moist gardens, greenhouses, and hammocks. (See the bibliography for particulars on tapes/CDs of anuran calls.)

Little information is available on the habits of most Florida frogs, toads, and treefrogs after they have left their breeding ponds.

Treefrogs of many species voice "rain calls," often from some height in trees, at the advent of spring and summer storms. These calls differ in tonal quality and structure from the advertisement calls heard at breeding sites.

Refer to the sections called "Abundance," "Habitat," and "Behavior" in each of the species accounts for particulars on each species.

# Salamanders and Newts (Caudata)

Salamanders and newts are attenuate, secretive creatures. Some found in Florida are so attenuate, they appear eel-like.

Florida salamanders fall naturally into six families, yet the members of those families are of more divergent appearance than the frogs, toads, and treefrogs.

Externally, adults of the mole salamanders, all but one of the lungless salamanders, and the newts look rather like smooth, scaleless, moist-skinned, clawless lizards. They are slender bodied and have short but fully functional legs and apparent tails. The single divergent lungless salamander is a permanent larva that retains external gills throughout its life, has no functional eyes, and lives in the perpetual blackness of caves. In general form, this creature looks much like a waterdog, but the waterdog has functional, though lidless, eyes.

The salamanders in the two remaining families are eel-like and aquatic. The amphiuma have no external gills and four *tiny* legs that are virtually useless for mobility. The sirens, on the other hand, have bushy external gills and two fully usable but small forelimbs. They lack hind limbs.

Most of Florida's salamanders have the normal two (or more) life stages, but some are neotenic (permanently aquatic larvae) or deposit terrestrial eggs in which direct development occurs.

Unlike the frogs, toads, and treefrogs of Florida, all of which have loud advertisement calls, salamanders are virtually voiceless. It is reported that some aquatic forms produce clicking sounds under water and yelping noises when restrained above water, but other than these rather inconsequential vocalizations, caudatans make no sounds. It is probable that they find each other by following scent trails (pheromones) with the tenacity of a prize bloodhound.

How to Find Salamanders and Newts in Florida

Salamanders might be said to be very much where you find them—and to find them, you must look carefully in the places they are.

Collectively, salamanders are among the most secretive of vertebrates, nor do many tolerate excessive heat.

Few, except cave-dwelling varieties for which day and night make little difference, are active during the hours of daylight. Rather, few emerge from their lairs until well after darkness. Even after nightfall, some wait-and-ambush predators sit with only their head and shoulders protruding from their burrows while quietly awaiting the arrival of a bug or worm.

To find amphiumas, sirens, and newts, look in the shallows of streams, reservoirs, ponds, or lakes. Unless you intend to net out and search through clumps of vegetation (a sometimes productive method of finding juveniles), look along the edges of these waters with a flashlight after dark. Search waterlogged leaf mats in streams for the larvae of brook salamanders and waterdogs.

Dusky and related salamanders forage at night along the edges of brooks and streams or sit on protruding rocks in the streams.

Some salamanders can be found by carefully turning streamside or ravine-side rocks or by rolling decomposing logs in the woodlands. Be sure to replace all ground cover you move.

Other salamanders can be found in the twilight zones of caves or other darkened areas, and one is restricted to ground water situations in the dark interiors of caves.

Remember that salamanders are delicate beasts. If you pick one up, do so carefully and with clean hands. Topical insecticides, sunscreen, and lotions and creams will quickly kill amphibians. Do not allow the salamanders to become warm or dry out.

When you have finished looking at or photographing it, put the salamander right back where you found it. Only in this way will one be there again when you wish to see it.

Florida's Frogs, Toads, and Other Amphibians

# 1

## Frogs, Toads, and Treefrogs

### A NOTE ABOUT TADPOLES

Tadpoles have internal gills, modified scraping mouthparts, and lack eyelids. Tadpoles grow, develops first hind legs, then forelegs, the tail is resorbed, eyelids develop, mouthparts alter, and within a period of weeks (sometimes months), tadpoles change into tiny, essentially terrestrial froglets. Newly metamorphosed frogs often are as difficult to identify as the tadpoles from which they transformed; however, within days identifying characteristics often become more apparent.

The identification of tadpoles is a discipline in itself. Tadpole appearance is mentioned in the text only if some readily visible species-unique characteristic is present.

### TOADS: FAMILY BUFONIDAE

**Taxonomic note:** The generic name of *Anaxyrus* has recently been proposed for the native Florida toads, and that of *Rhinella* for the introduced cane toad. Since this proposal remains controversial, we will continue to use the long-established name of *Bufo* for all toads.

There are few persons who do not recognize a toad, commonly called a "hop-toad." Most toads have a rather dry-appearing warty skin and, except while breeding, inhabit relatively dry habitats. There are four species of toads in Florida, ranging in size from the very large introduced giant toad to the very small oak toad.

The length of anurans is determined by measuring the distance between the tip of the snout and the vent. This is termed snout-vent length and is abbreviated SVL.

Florida's four toad species all have prominent toxin-secreting parotoid (shoulder) glands. The secreted toxins may vary from distasteful (produced by the three native species) to the potentially lethal secretions of the Latin American giant toad. When frightened (especially by predatory mammals, e.g., a dog, fox, cat, skunk, raccoon) a toad may arch its back and tilt its head downward. In this defensive position, the parotoid glands are foremost, and the toad may butt its enemy, exuding and smearing the secretions from the glands, thereby deterring the predator.

Except for the oak toad, which lays its eggs singly or in short strings, all Florida species lay their eggs in long paired strings.

Fowler's toad

Southern toad

Oak toad

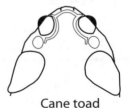

Cane toad

## A Toad in the Hand and None in the Field

Florida is a state with four toads. Three—the southern, oak, and Fowler's toads—are native, and one, the cane (or giant or marine toad), is a pet trade introduction. Three of the four species are very easy to find, but finding the fourth, the Fowler's toad, is usually a lesson in exasperation at best and an exercise in absolute futility at worst.

Failure to find a Fowler's toad in Florida would seem a personal failure on my part. The toad is not known to be rare, and Fowler's toad has a huge range in Florida: almost the entire panhandle. It does seem to have changed its habitat preference in Florida. North of the Sunshine State, Fowler's toad is often (probably even usually) associated with open, sandy habitats. It can be common to abundant along pond edges, near marshes, and in sandy riparian situations.

In Florida, though, Fowler's toad seems to prefer riparian forestlands, habitats with a richer soil than you would expect for them farther north.

It had been some time since I had thought about Fowler's toad in Florida, and I had never looked specifically for one. The first (and only) time I had seen them, Patti and I had been up in the Florida Caverns region looking for Georgia blind salamanders. We found one of those, took some pictures, looked at flowers, learned that purple was a favorite color of one of the park rangers, and by the time evening came around, we were on our way home, retracing the same convoluted route that had carried us first northward and then westward. There were no GPSs then, and although we had maps aplenty, our course always just seemed to wander as we plied our way along country roads.

We were plying when from out of the darkness came a loud "waaahhh." I braked. An answering waaahhh came from another point, then another and another. Fowler's toads. I remember thinking then that I hadn't heard the species since leaving New England several decades earlier. But neither had I really looked for the toads in Florida. They were common in New England; that they were common here seemed borne out by our stumbling discovery that night. I photographed one and we left.

You can probably guess the rest of this tale. Yes, you're right. Despite dedicated searches between then and now, we've never found another Fowler's toad in Florida.

The moral, I guess, is that you should never take anything from the natural world for granted. What happens once may never happen again.

# 1. Fowler's Toad

*Bufo fowleri*

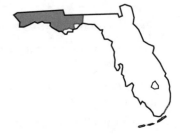

**Size:** This is a fairly large, robust toad. Females may exceed 3½ inches SVL, but males are apt to be somewhat smaller.

**Identification:** The Fowler's toad is usually gray, more rarely a grayish brown but, unlike the southern toad, never red. Fowler's toads have dark dorsal and lateral spots of irregular shape neatly outlined in very light gray. There are usually 3 or more warts in each dark spot. The interorbital crests never bear large posterior knobs. The venter is light and usually has no, or little, dark pigmentation.

Males have dark throats year-round and a single large subgular vocal sac.

The tadpoles are small, black dorsally, white ventrally and have narrow unpigmented tail fins.

**Voice:** Calling males produce a loud, unmusical, nasal, waaaaaah while sitting on open sandy banks, usually within a few inches of the waterline.

**Habitat/Range:** In Florida, Fowler's toad is a species of the bottomlands of the western panhandle.

**Abundance:** This species is uncommon in Florida.

**Behavior:** Like most toads, the Fowler's moves in short hops. They are secretive, and usually hide by day beneath ground debris or in a burrow of their own making. They become active at dusk and are often found after dark beneath porch lights and streetlights where tired insects fall, crawl—and get eaten.

**Reproduction:** Fowler's toads often breed in lakes, ponds, and ditches where water retention is quite stable; however, they also use temporarily flooded bottomland sites. They often breed a little later in the spring than the southern toad. Double gelatinous strings of eggs are laid by floating amplexed females. Clutches of up to 8,000 eggs have been reported.

**Similar species:** Differentiating toad species can be challenging, particularly if the toad is not fully adult. Hybrids do occur and can be difficult to ID.

In the western Florida panhandle, three toad species occur sympatrically. They are easily differentiated by call. Fowler's toads voice a nasal waaaah, southern toads produce a high-pitched, rapidly pulsed trill, and oak toads make a chicklike peep. Hybrids between Fowler's and southern toads produce an intermediate whirring trill.

Oak toads are small (1¼ inches SVL) and lack a prominent knob at the rear of each interorbital crest. Adult southern toads have a greatly developed knob at the posterior end of each interorbital crest. Southern toads may be red in color; if dark spots are present, the spots often contain only one large wart. In general, southern toads appear smoother skinned (having fewer tubercles) than Fowler's toads. The eastern spadefoot has vertically elliptical pupils.

**Comments:** Records indicate the Fowler's toad has never been very common in Florida. Throughout its Florida range the Fowler's toad is vastly outnumbered by the sympatric southern toad. Careful monitoring of known populations and life history studies in Florida would be of great benefit to biologists.

# 2. Cane (Giant) Toad

*Bufo marinus*

**Size:** Populations of this toad in Florida seem to now vary in the adult size attained. Specimens with an SVL of 6–7 inches are still regularly found in the Miami, Homestead, and Florida City area and can be quite startling to someone unfamiliar with this toad. Most of those seen in the Tarpon Springs area in recent years are reproducing when in the range of 3–4 inches. We speculate that the size reduction of this northernmost population is brought about by cooler winter temperatures than optimum for this tropical species as well as a winter reduction in available food items. Females are by far the larger sex.

**Identification:** This immense toad varies between brown and red in ground color. It may or may not have darker and lighter spots and marblings. Females are more heavily patterned than males. The body tubercles of breeding males are tipped with tiny spines. The parotoid glands are immense and extend far down onto the shoulders. The cranial crests are prominent, but the interorbital pair have no bulbous posterior projections.

Males have a comparatively small (but still very visible) subgular vocal sac and call while sitting on the shore or in shallow water.

Tadpoles are black above and light (often speckled with black) ventrally.

**Voice:** A low-pitched, slowly pulsed, rattling trill is voiced by males. The largest males have the deepest voices.

# 3. Oak Toad

*Bufo quercicus*

**Size:** Oak toads are adult at an SVL of ¾ inch (males) to 1 inch (females). Occasional females may attain a length of 1¼ inches.

**Identification:** This tiny toad may be very dark when cold but rather brightly colored and well patterned with paired, light-edged dark dorsal spots when warm. The ground color is some shade of brown to gray. At all times a prominent white, yellow, or orange vertebral stripe is visible. The warts are variable in color but may be russet, red, orange, or yellow.

The venter is light. Males have a dark throat that swells into an enormous, anteriorly projecting ("sausage-shaped") vocal sac when the toad is calling.

The parotoid gland is prominent and elongate. The cranial crests, while present, are not well defined. The posterior ends of the interorbital crests angle inward to form a weakly defined L.

The tiny tadpoles are dark above and lighter below. The upper tail fin is spotted with dark pigment; the lower tail fin is not.

**Voice:** The call of this toad is unlike that of any other Florida bufonid. Males produce a rapidly repeated, strident peeping that can be almost overpowering when large choruses are heard.

**Habitat/Range:** The oak toad is associated with well-drained, sandy oak-pine scrublands, habitats that are disappearing rapidly in Florida. The oak toad can be heard vocalizing, sometimes in deafening choruses, in flooded roadside drainage ditches bisecting oak-pine habitats.

**Abundance:** Although seemingly less common than once, the oak toad remains common to abundant in many areas of Florida. It does not seem to persist long in urban and suburban areas but may remain common in agricultural areas.

**Behavior:** The oak toad may be encountered foraging in shady areas even on the hottest summer days. It may be inactive during the winter months. Although males may call sporadically during daylight hours (especially on overcast or rainy days), the largest and most persistent breeding choruses are heard on humid or rainy summer nights.

**Reproduction:** Oak toads utilize shallow semipermanent ponds, temporary flatwoods ponds, and roadside drainage ditches for breeding. The 100–250 eggs are laid singly or in very short strings. Eggs float on the water surface or adhere to vegetation with which they come in contact.

**Similar species:** The peeping vocalizations of this toad are distinctive. Juvenile toads of other species usually do not have the prominent light vertebral line or well-developed parotoid glands.

**Comments:** The shrill calls of this toad are frequently mistaken for bird calls. Oak toads blend remarkably with the grasses from which they often call, and finding them can be difficult.

# 4. Southern Toad

*Bufo terrestris*

**Size:** Female southern toads are substantially larger than males. Males are adult at 2–3 inches while females occasionally exceed 4½ inches SVL.

**Identification:** This is Florida's most variable toad. The ground color can be gray, brown, red, or nearly charcoal. Dark dorsal spots may or may not be present. If present, the spots may be well or weakly defined and each often contains one or two (sometimes more) warts. A vestige of a lateral stripe is often visible. The venter is light but usually variably pigmented with black spots or flecks. The parotoid glands are kidney shaped.

Males have a dark throat and a large, rounded vocal sac. Males call while sitting in exposed areas of the shoreline (occasionally in short grasses) or in very shallow water.

The small tadpoles are black above and dark below. The upper tail fin is more heavily pigmented than the lower.

**Voice:** The voice of the southern toad is a penetrating, high-pitched, rapidly pulsed trill. Large choruses can be uncomfortably overpowering.

**Habitat/Range:** The southern toad is a habitat generalist. It may be encountered in urban backyards, along lake and pond shores, in wooded hammocks, in highland scrub, and in all habitats between. It can be found in every county in Florida.

**Abundance:** This is the most abundant and frequently seen toad in Florida. Possibly because it is eaten or otherwise outcompeted by the introduced cane toad, the southern toad is hard to find on the southern peninsula in regions where the cane toad is common.

**Behavior:** This is the common backyard hop-toad of Florida. Although it may be active diurnally during overcast or rainy weather, the southern toad is primarily nocturnal. It occurs in most areas but seems most common where sandy soils provide rapid drainage. This toad forages beneath porch lights and street lights to dine on falling insects.

**Reproduction:** Southern toads lay dual strings of eggs at the edges of both permanent and ephemeral ponds, lakes, ditches, backyard lily pools, and canals. A female may lay more than 4,000 eggs.

**Similar species:** Although juveniles can be difficult to positively identify, the adult of no other Florida toad species has such prominent cranial crests and interorbital knobs.

**Comments:** The southern toad remains a commonly seen species. When climatic conditions are suitable in the spring, large numbers gather to breed. These congregations may happen literally overnight. Following the breeding season, they disperse widely, and the few seen after that give no indication of the true numbers in a given area.

## GREENHOUSE FROGS: FAMILY
## ELEUTHERODACTYLIDAE

The two representatives of this family in Florida are both alien species. The coqui is a very cold-sensitive species that is tenuously established at best. The greenhouse frog is firmly established.

These two species are the only frogs in our state that undergo direct development in the egg. Since there is no free-swimming tadpole stage, neither the coqui nor the greenhouse frog is dependent on standing water for breeding.

These frogs lack webbing between the toes.

# 5. Puerto Rican Coqui

*Eleutherodactylus coqui*

**Size:** Although coquis are known to attain 2¼ inches SVL in Puerto Rico, those in Florida seem adult at 1¼–1¾ inches long.

**Identification:** The ground color of the coqui varies from grayish brown through tan to rich brown, either with or without a pattern. If a pattern is present, it may be obscure or prominent. Many specimens have a dark W-shaped marking discernible above the forelimbs. A light dorsolateral stripe may be present. A broad, light interorbital bar is often present. This species has large digital disks.

The venter is primarily light but often has scattered dark blotches or spots. Males have a large, rounded subgular vocal sac.

**Voice:** This species has derived its common name from its two-syllabled call of "co-QUI," with the accent on the last syllable.

**Habitat/Range:** In Puerto Rico, this is an arboreal frog known to climb to canopy positions. Those we have watched in Florida have, for the most part, remained fairly close to the ground (6 inches to 7 feet up). We have found males calling from the trunks of citrus and ornamental shade trees

## Warbles and Whistles, A Tale of Two Frogs

The two calls, both from elfin frogs, couldn't have been more different. The call of the one was so soft and tinkling that if you didn't know it was the voice of a frog, you'd likely think the sound was that of a small garden insect, while the call of the other was loud, two syllabled, and shrill. Despite the fact that the calls were very dissimilar, somewhere in their lineage these small frogs were related. Both were alien species, one from the Bahamas and Cuba and the other from Puerto Rico, and both laid their eggs in damp terrestrial situations, not requiring water to breed (the only frogs in Florida to breed in this manner). While the Bahaman species was so widely and successfully distributed in Florida that it seemed native, the Puerto Rican species was known from only a few locales on the southern peninsula and was so erratic in its occurrence that researchers often wondered whether it really did occur in Florida. I could not help but wonder while listening to these two frogs about the physiological quirks or differences that allowed one to be so successful in its adopted Florida home while the other found colonization of the Sunshine State so fraught with difficulty that it had never been able to expand its range. Was it Florida's winter temperatures alone, or were other factors involved?

The frog that was producing the tinkling tones was the very successful greenhouse frog, *Eleutherodactylus planirostris*, and the loud calls were those of the very localized coqui, *Eleutherodactylus coqui*.

The greenhouse frog seems to have hit the shores of Florida and, except for stopping long enough to breed and expand its populations, to never have really stopped running. It is now an abundant species throughout most of Florida. It *might* still be absent from a couple of anuran-inhospitable locales, but overall Florida has been its oyster (or its fruitfly). The presence or absence of the greenhouse frog can be easily confirmed during humid warm weather by its weak, tinkling, insectlike calls that are often voiced from shady irrigated gardens or lawns.

On the other hand, although it was first reported from Florida in the mid-1900s, the continued presence of the coqui as a feral entity in the state in 2009 is now tenuous. It has proven much more cold sensitive than the greenhouse frog, and the well-documented population at Fairchild Tropical Botanic Gardens was eradicated by a cold snap in the mid-1970s. Following the disappearance of that population, the coqui has been documented in the

*continued*

Homestead-Florida City region, where it has always been most prevalent at plant nurseries. A question that has often been posed, but never satisfactorily answered, pertains to the actual status of the coqui in Florida: do a few of these little frogs actually survive Florida's periodic cold snaps and breed, or are the populations continually replenished by eggs (and adults?) imported in plants from Puerto Rico?

I can only say that there are times when the strident "co-QUI" calls cannot be heard for weeks or months on end in Florida, while at other times it impossible to miss the vocalizations.

as well as from the leaves of both epiphytic and terrestrial bromeliads. This frog is known from Miami, Homestead, and Florida City.

**Abundance:** This is a rare and local species in Florida. It is known to exist only in and around a few greenhouses in southern Miami-Dade County. Although it has been seen and heard in Florida for well over a decade, the fact that it remains very localized and seems unable to expand its range causes us to consider its presence here tenuous. Even where present in some numbers, this frog is seldom seen except at night.

**Behavior:** Except on strongly overcast or rainy days when it may be active, the coqui retires to the seclusion of rock piles or ground debris or the axils of bromeliad leaves during the day. Both sexes are active at night, and males are *very* vocal on rainy days and after dark.

**Reproduction:** In Puerto Rico, the coqui breeds year-round. Little is known about the reproductive biology of this frog in Florida, but breeding activities here may be most heavily skewed toward our very hot, humid, and often unstable late spring, summer, and early autumn weather. One to two dozen eggs are laid in moisture-retaining pockets amid ground debris or, occasionally, in protected elevated sites. Males tend the clutches from deposition until shortly after hatching. There is no free-swimming tadpole stage. For a few days after hatching, coquis have a tail nub.

**Similar species:** The greenhouse frog is smaller, more slender, and, although variable, usually of a rusty dorsal coloration. See also the species account and photograph of the squirrel treefrog (account 16).

**Comments:** Although it could once be found in some numbers amid the tropical plantings at Fairchild Tropical Gardens in south Miami, the coqui seems no longer to occur there. If current information is accurate, the coqui is now restricted to about a half-dozen or fewer bromeliad nursery/greenhouses in south Dade County. Whether the populations are self-sustaining even in the artificiality of these habitats is unknown. It may be that new coquis and their eggs, arriving in bromeliad shipments from Puerto Rico, replenish the populations.

## 6. Greenhouse Frog

*Eleutherodactylus planirostris*

**Size:** Male greenhouse frogs are adult at about ¾ inch SVL, but occasionally grow slightly larger. Females, which may be slightly larger than 1 inch SVL, are more robust than the males.

**Identification:** The dorsum of the greenhouse frogs bears either a mottled or a lineate pattern. No matter which phase is at hand, mixtures of rust to orange and brown make up the dorsal and lateral colors. The venter is usually an off-white but may be gray. The skin is warty.

Males call on rainy days or at night from the seclusion of garden plants or woodland herbs. They may call while on the ground amid leaf litter or while sitting several inches above the ground on the leaves of plants.

Despite the presence of a subgular vocal sac, the calls have little carrying power.

**Voice:** Greenhouse frogs produce a varied series of insectlike chirps and trills. The calls of this species are very apt to be mistaken for those of a cricket or other garden insect.

**Habitat/Range:** This is a ubiquitous species. It can be found in yards, woodlands, scrub, and other diverse habitats throughout Florida. It is native to Cuba and the Bahamas. Greenhouse frogs are particularly common in Florida in gardens, greenhouses, nurseries, and wherever else occasional sprinkling prevents a complete drying of the substrate. They seek seclusion beneath boards, mulch, fallen leaves, or stepping stones and are adept at gaining quick access to the smallest of crevices and cracks.

**Abundance:** Although a decidedly tropical species adversely impacted by cold temperatures, the introduced greenhouse frog has become firmly established and slowly extended its range northward. It is now found throughout Florida.

**Behavior:** This little frog thrives in settings as diverse as urban gardens and pristine woodlands. It is one of the most secretive of frogs. After having dwelt with greenhouse frogs in our yard for more than 40 years, we have not yet seen a male vocalizing; as we near their hiding places, they fall silent and remain so until we leave. These frogs are active on warm, heavily overcast or rainy days, but are essentially nocturnal.

**Reproduction:** In Florida the greenhouse frog breeds during the hot days of late spring, summer, and early autumn. One to two dozen eggs are laid in moisture-retaining debris or damp pockets of earth. Full metamorphosis occurs in the egg capsules. The tiny froglets emerge with a tail nub but are otherwise minuscule replicas of the adults

**Similar species:** Spring peepers may be pinkish but usually have a dark X on the back. Other chorus frogs are associated with marshes and pond edges and have a lineate pattern of dark spots or stripes. Cricket frogs and squirrel treefrogs have extensive webbing on the hind feet.

**Comments:** This tiny frog was introduced into Florida from the West Indies. It has proven to be a very successful species.

## HYLID FROGS: FAMILY HYLIDAE

### Treefrog Musings

I was sitting on the back deck late yesterday afternoon, musing and watching a "dance of the gnats" in a beam of the setting sun. Hundreds of little midges whirled, swirled, and darted about in what seemed utter abandon. What, I wondered, was the reason for such a midge congregation? Eventually, as the position of the sun changed and the gnats became difficult to see, I glanced in another direction and noticed, resting quietly atop a window

*continued*

frame, just beneath a porch light, all hunkered down with legs folded tightly against its body, a green treefrog. More musing (read, I had found another excuse not to get up and do something constructive).

One of the dogs came over and lay down beside me. The world continued its inexorable rotation, and dusk enveloped Dog and me. A bat—probably a Mexican freetail—twisted and turned in pursuit of insects. Within moments it was joined by several others. The gnat dance had changed to a bat dance. I wondered whether the bats would bother with insects as small as those midges? A southbound nighthawk *peeeent*ed in the gathering darkness.

I glanced at the treefrog again. Sensing darkness was nearing, it had sat up and seemed to be looking around. I decided to help it find dinner. I turned the porch light on, and within a few seconds small moths were drawn in. The treefrog seemed pleased.

Excluding the spring peepers (since they start calling in late November down here, I have always contended they should be called winter peepers), which never seem to leave the vicinity of the swampland in which they breed, green treefrogs are the most common hylid in the area. From late spring through midsummer they call lustily and nightly—rain or shine—from a nearby swampland. Then they disperse, and some manage to make it across a busily traveled four lanes of tarmac to take up residency in our yard until the next spring draws them once again to their breeding sites. The treefrogs don't have the same site fidelity as, say, a tiger salamander, for the journeys of a few always seem to end at our little turtle pond, where they sing the season through. Occasionally a male waylays a female at the turtle pond, and we are able to watch the development of a few eggs and tadpoles.

Then as I watched the feeding green treefrog, I began wondering, what havoc would be wreaked on native hylid populations by the recent arrival of the Cuban treefrog in our area? As far as I knew, the first example of this large, voracious treefrog (females have attained 5 inches in length) had been found in this area about six years earlier (2004). Since the reporting of that first interloper, more have been found each year.

The Cuban treefrogs have shown they can withstand a colder than usual winter in north central Florida. Somehow it seems that change is not only forthcoming but inevitable.

The hylid frogs of Florida, the cricket, tree, and chorus frogs, are contained in five genera. Within these genera, there are 16 species (3 with two subspecies each) of which 14 are native. Of the two remaining species, one, the Cuban treefrog, is a firmly established alien species, and the other, the Australian great green treefrog, may now have been extirpated from Florida.

The cricket frogs (2 species, one of which has 2 subspecies) are of variable color, usually found near water, and, having only vestigial toe pads, do not readily climb. Both are tiny species that attain a length of barely an inch. They have fully webbed hind feet, a dark interorbital triangle, and distinctive striping on the hidden surface of the thigh. To see the striping, the frogs must be caught and their legs gently extended.

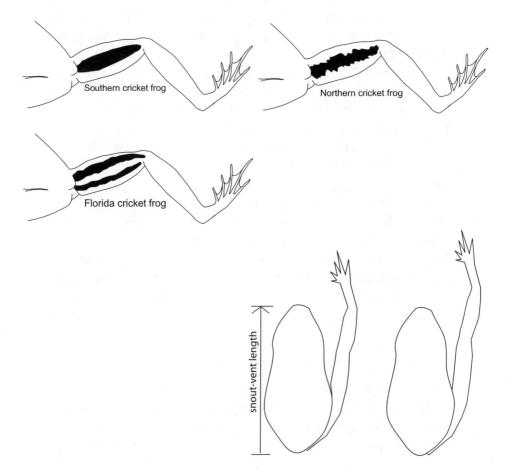

Southern cricket frog

Northern cricket frog

Florida cricket frog

snout-vent length

The treefrogs (9 species, none of which are subspeciated) all have toe pads and are capable of climbing. Although most species may not often climb to treetop height, a few do so. The treefrogs are of variable size, ranging from the slender 1-inch length of the pine woods treefrog to the hefty 5 inches attained by the female Cuban treefrog. The largest native treefrog species is the barking treefrog, with SVL of 2¼ inches. The amount of webbing on the hind feet varies but is usually considerable. Hybridization occurs. Most species and some hybrids are easily identified in the field both by appearance and by voice.

For the most part, the chorus frogs (5 species, 2 with 2 subspecies each) are also small frogs. The largest species in Florida is the relatively robust ornate chorus frog. The chorus frogs have very small toe pads and, although capable of climbing, except for the spring peeper, seldom do so. The toes bear only basal webbing. Of the chorus frogs, only the spring peeper is recognized by most folks. It is the most "treefrog-like" member of the genus.

All Florida hylids can be field identified by their distinctive breeding calls. The clicking calls of the two species of cricket frogs are the most confusingly similar. Although we have tried to describe the sounds made by each, anuran vocalizations do not lend themselves well to words. To learn these, we recommend you obtain the CD of *The Calls of Frogs and Toads of Eastern and Central North America*, by the Lang Elliott Nature Sound Studio.

All Florida hylids breed in "normal" fashion. The two sexes encounter each other in breeding ponds, streams, or bogs. Females normally respond to the species-specific calls of the males, but, as already mentioned, hybridization does occasionally occur. Males grasp the females behind the forelimbs in a breeding embrace termed "axillary amplexus." The eggs are fertilized as they are laid and hatch into tadpoles within a few days.

## Cricket Frogs: Genus *Acris*

Although not difficult to identify to genus, these frogs are often difficult to differentiate to species. Cricket frogs as a group essentially lack toe pads, have a dark triangular or V-shaped mark between the eyes, and have striping on the hidden surface of the thighs. The southern and the northern chorus frogs have numerous tiny papillae on both sides of the vent. These papillae are absent in the Florida cricket frog.

Cricket frogs may be heard calling sporadically during cool weather, but they are actually hot-weather breeders.

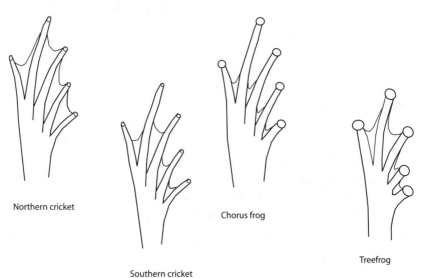

Northern cricket

Chorus frog

Southern cricket

Treefrog

# 7. Northern Cricket Frog

*Acris crepitans crepitans*

**Size:** A minuscule frog, the northern cricket frog is fully adult at from 1 to 1¼ inches SVL. Females may be marginally the larger and more robust gender.

**Identification:** This tiny, warty, agile frog is variably colored and patterned. The ground color can be brown, tan, charcoal, of some shade of green, or various combinations of these colors. The markings, usually oriented longitudinally, can be yellow, green, russet, or brown. The single broad thigh stripe is usually irregularly edged. Anal papillae are present. Cricket frogs can be differentiated in part by the comparative length of their hind leg; that of the northern is comparatively short. If it is gently extended and drawn forward (adpressed), the heel usually does not extend beyond the snout. A dark interorbital triangle is present. The webbing of the toes is extensive, reaching the tips of all except the longest toe. Males have a dark throat skin that distends into a single large subgular vocal sac.

Tadpoles in advanced stages of development are dark dorsally and have a pinkish venter and a dark tail tip.

**Voice:** The initial notes in the lengthy sequence of clicking calls produced by the northern cricket frog are slower and more distinct from the next note than those toward the end. The sound produced by a large chorus is harsh and shrilly discordant.

**Habitat/Range:** The northern cricket frog is associated with permanent water sources and is particularly common in, but not restricted to, sunny shallows matted with sphagnum and emergent plants such as frogsbit and lizard's tail. Although it ranges widely in the eastern United States, the northern cricket frog occurs in Florida only in the panhandle from Leon County westward.

**Abundance:** This frog can be quite common in shallow-water habitats.

**Behavior:** Although they may sit atop floating or pondside mosses in patches of sunlight for long periods, northern cricket frogs are alert and agile when approached. While it may seem there is no rhyme or reason to their long, erratic hops, these frogs are remarkably successful at avoiding capture.

**Reproduction:** The several small clusters of eggs are attached to submerged plants. A complete clutch comprises 100–200 eggs, a small number compared with those of some frog species.

**Similar species:** When the two species of cricket frogs are compared, the northern cricket frog has the shorter nose and shorter legs than the southern. When closely compared, the northern species can be termed "chunky," while the southern cricket frog might be called streamlined and lithe. The extent of webbing of the toes and shape of thigh stripe are the most constant differences. (See species account 8 for a description of the southern cricket frog.) Chorus frogs have reduced webbing on the toes, and treefrogs have discernible toe pads.

**Comments:** These tiny frogs are quick to take fright if approached incautiously. If an observer sits quietly (often difficult to do amid the clouds of mosquitoes also found in these habitats), the cricket frogs will usually reassemble and may even start chorusing.

# 8. Southern Cricket Frog

*Acris gryllus gryllus*

Southern cricket frog ■
Florida cricket frog ▢

**Size:** This frog is fully adult at from ¾ to 1 inch SVL.

**Identification:** A great variability in both ground color and dorsal pattern typifies this warty, alert, and agile hylid. The ground color runs the gamut from a rather deep brown through tan and russet to green. The frog is darkest when cold. A dark diagonal bar is often present on each lower side. If a vertebral marking is present, it is weak, but the dorsolateral and lateral markings are well defined. Males have dark throats and a single subgular vocal sac. The single light-edged dark thigh stripe has rather even edges. Anal papillae are present.

The legs are long (if gently and carefully adpressed along the body, the heel extends beyond the tip of the snout). The webbing does not reach the tips of any toes.

**Voice:** The clicking vocalizations are more metallic than those of the northern cricket frog and produced in a series of 1–7 or 8 rapidly repeated notes.

**Habitat/Range:** In Florida this subspecies is found only in the northwestern panhandle. Potholes, ponds, lakes, bogs, marshes, and open sphagnum-bog swamp edges are among the habitats utilized by this moisture-loving frog, which is often particularly common where extensive mats of sphagnum exist. The frogs blend remarkably with that substrate.

**Abundance:** This is a common cricket frog, often found in dense populations.

**Behavior:** Alert, active, agile, and normally unapproachable all describe the Florida cricket frog. This little frog explodes into a series of long, frenzied jumps when approached.

**Reproduction:** Several small clusters of eggs are deposited. They are attached to submerged vegetation. From 100 to 200 eggs are laid.
**Similar species:** The northern cricket frog has shorter hind limbs, and the hind foot webbing extends to the tips of all but the longest toe. Chorus frogs have very reduced webbing on the toes.
**Subspecies**

9. Florida Cricket Frog, *Acris gryllus dorsalis,* is of very similar appearance but has two dark stripes on the hidden surface of each thigh and lacks anal papillae. Except for the northwestern panhandle, this subspecies is found throughout the state.

## Treefrogs: Genera *Hyla, Osteopilus,* and *Pelodryas*

With the possible exception of the very variable squirrel treefrog, which has a green phase that can be mistaken for a stripeless green treefrog and a brown phase resembling a pine woods treefrog, all Florida hylids are easily identifiable in the field. They vary in size, color, webbing, habitat preference, breeding season, and much else. The same frog can undergo chameleonlike changes of color, being brown or heavily patterned one moment and green or unpatterned a short time later. This is especially notable for the barking treefrog. Cold treefrogs are often very dark in coloration. Most treefrogs are easily approached on overcast or, especially, rainy nights, when they are at their breeding sites. Except when they are vocalizing, their presence may be unsuspected.

# 10. Pine Barrens Treefrog

*Hyla andersonii*

**Size:** In Florida, Pine Barrens treefrogs seem slightly smaller than those in the Carolinas and New Jersey. Adults in the Florida populations are usually between 1¼ and 1½ inches in SVL.

**Identification:** If not the most beautiful treefrog in America, the Pine Barrens treefrog surely runs a close second to whichever species you may personally favor. Unless cold or stressed, when it may be an unremarkable olive green, *H. andersonii* varies from jade to leaf green dorsally. A broad plum to lavender stripe extends rearward from the nostril, through the eye and tympanum, to the groin. This is bordered dorsally with cream or yellow. The hands and feet are also purplish. Orange spots and a paler orange suffusion appear on the posterior sides, beneath the legs, and in the groin. Except for where it is suffused with orange, the venter is white. Males have a dark throat that distends when the frog is vocalizing into a rounded subgular vocal sac.

The tadpoles are olive green with dark flecking on body and tail.

**Voice:** The call of this species is often likened to the honking of a goose; however, the calls of the Florida populations are higher pitched than those of northern populations. The notes are an oft repeated, high-pitched "quonk."

**Habitat/Range:** In Florida, the Pine Barrens treefrog is found only in hillside seepage bogs. These are uncommon habitats known to exist only in a few areas in the western panhandle. Titi, red maple, fetterbush, sedges, insectivorous plants, and sphagnum are among the plant species associated with these bogs.

**Abundance:** This is an uncommon, localized, and highly specialized treefrog. It is a protected species in Florida.

**Behavior:** The secretive Pine Barrens treefrog breeds during the spring and summer. Once the breeding populations have dispersed, this frog is seldom seen.

**Reproduction:** Small clusters of eggs are deposited in shallow water. A total number of 150–250 eggs seems the normal complement. The egg clusters adhere to submerged vegetation.

**Similar species:** The green treefrog is often found in the same steepheads as the Pine Barrens treefrog. The green treefrog is larger and more slender and lacks orange on the venter; if a lateral stripe is present, it is metallic white.

**Comments:** Pine Barrens treefrogs occasionally hybridize with pine woods and green treefrogs.

# 11. Western Bird-voiced Treefrog

*Hyla avivoca avivoca*

**Size:** This treefrog may attain 1¾ inches SVL but is usually smaller. Females are marginally larger than males.

**Identification:** The dorsal coloration varies from pale or pea green through gray to charcoal. The same frog can be greenish at one moment and deep gray soon thereafter. Cold or stressed specimens are usually the darkest. A large, dark central figure (narrowly outlined with charcoal or black) is usually visible on the back. Leg bars and a dark interorbital marking are present. The groin and concealed surfaces of the hind legs are greenish or a very pale yellow but never bright orange. Males have a dark throat and a subgular vocal sac. A dark-edged, white to yellowish green spot, usually wider than high, is beneath each eye.

The tadpoles are buff or light brown with a reddish or rose saddle and rose to pink fins.

**Voice:** The calls are melodious flutelike whistles that have been likened to the ululations produced by some birds or of a person whistling for a dog.

**Habitat/Range:** The western bird-voiced treefrog is a denizen of the great southern tupelo and sweetgum river swamps. In Florida it is encountered from Leon County westward on the panhandle.

**Abundance:** In suitable habitat this is a common to abundant treefrog.

**Behavior:** Once it has left the breeding sites, little is known about the life history of this treefrog. Adults have been found as they cross roadways during late summer nighttime showers, and new metamorphs have been found on swamp-edge roadways in September. This species typically choruses once the muggy nights of late spring and summer have set in but may vocalize as early as late March when periodic coolness can still be expected. Autumn showers may also induce sporadic vocalizations. Chorusing males typically call from high in trees in the late afternoon but then descend to calling stations 2–6 feet above the surface of the water once darkness has fallen.

**Reproduction:** This small treefrog may lay several hundred eggs. The eggs are deposited in clusters of 10–30 and adhere to surface or submerged vegetation.

**Similar species:** The larger Cope's gray treefrog has orange rather than green or yellow in the groin and on the hind legs. The pine woods treefrog lacks a white blotch beneath the eye.

# 12. Cope's Gray Treefrog

*Hyla chrysoscelis*

**Size:** Large females of this robust species may attain 2¼ inches SVL. Males are somewhat smaller.

**Identification:** Gray treefrogs are capable of undergoing chameleonlike changes from pale or pea green through many shades of gray to charcoal. Cold or stressed frogs are often the darkest. A large and intricate darker dorsal figure is usually prominently visible, outlined in black. Leg bars and an interorbital bar are usually present. The interorbital bar may be broken midway. The groin and undersurface of the hind legs are orange yellow to bright orange. The rear of the thighs is orange patterned with black reticulations.

A dark-edged white spot, often taller than wide, is present beneath each eye. Males have dark throats and a large, round subgular vocal sac.

The attractive tadpole of this species is buff or gold with a rose tail fin.

**Voice:** The call of this species consists of a loud, resonant, high-pitched, rapid trill that is not dissimilar to the call of a red-bellied woodpecker. The chosen calling station is often one to several feet above the water. It may call while sitting on a limb or choose to cling head-up or head-down to the trunk of a fairly large tree. Gray treefrogs may be heard in full chorus from late March or early April to June or July and may call sporadically for several months thereafter.

**Habitat/Range:** This treefrog prefers wet woodland habitats where it breeds in pools and swamps. It is widely distributed across the northern third of the Florida peninsula and is known from all the panhandle counties.

**Abundance:** Although common to abundant, unless vocalizing, Cope's gray treefrog is an easily overlooked hylid.

**Behavior:** The gray treefrog is strongly arboreal and quite apt to vocalize during summer storms from much higher in the trees than many other hylids. It is common near the periphery of woodland ponds and swamps but also calls from deep in swampy situations.

**Reproduction:** Females may lay more than 1,500 eggs. They are deposited in small clusters and may adhere to surface or submerged vegetation or float free.

**Similar species:** In Florida, only the western bird-voiced treefrog is apt to be mistaken for this species; it has a greenish or pale yellow rather than an orange wash in its groin and on the underside of its hind limbs.

**Comments:** Florida is one of the few states in which the taxonomy and identification of the gray treefrog doesn't seem problematic. The visually identical tetraploid species *Hyla versicolor* (*H. chrysoscelis* is diploid) is not known to be present in Florida.

# 13. Green Treefrog

*Hyla cinerea*

**Size:** The green treefrog is adult at a slender 1¾–2¼ inches in length. Females are a little larger than the males.

**Identification:** Low temperature and/or stress produce a dorsal coloration of olive brown to dark olive green. Sleeping green treefrogs may be olive tan, but when these little frogs are alert and relatively content, they are a beautiful bright to forest green and among the prettiest of the hylids. The throat of male green treefrogs is green on the sides and yellowish green to yellowish white centrally. The distended subgular vocal sac is lighter in color than the sides of the throat. The venter is white. Green treefrogs often have an enamel white lateral stripe extending from the tip of the snout to the groin. On some specimens the line may be incomplete or entirely lacking. A white femoral and heel stripe is often present. Small but well-defined gold or orange dorsal spots may be present.

The tadpoles are rather nondescript, being olive to greenish with a yellowish stripe extending from nostril to eye.

**Voice:** The calls are a loud rather unmusical series of "quonks." The frequently repeated single notes of this treefrog have been likened by some listeners to the peals of distant cowbells. The frogs often call from a foot or so above the water on the leaves of emergent arrowheads or similar vegetation. Occasionally they call from water level while sitting on floating vegetation. They may be heard chorusing in Florida from early February (temperatures permitting) to late summer. They call most continually on warm overcast nights.

**Habitat/Range:** By day green treefrogs are occasionally encountered resting, eyes tightly closed, on emergent or pondside vegetation. It is a common "backyard species" over much of Florida and often drawn to porch lights to feed on insects. Green treefrogs are associated with more open areas than many other hylids and are common around cattle tanks, pasture ponds, slowly flowing canals, lakes, and like areas with a profusion of low herbaceous growth. At night they hunt and call while sitting on the leaves of cattails, arrowheads, and other such emergents. It is found throughout Florida, including the Keys.

**Abundance:** Not only is this one of the most beautiful of Florida's treefrogs, it is one of the most abundant as well.

**Behavior:** This frog often strays from the breeding ponds into open woodlands or backyards during the day. There it is commonly seen hunkered down, legs drawn tightly to the body and eyes closed, on the foliage of broad-leafed plants or on walls. Green treefrogs are capable jumpers but often walk unless frightened.

**Reproduction:** The complement of 400–600 eggs is laid in numerous clusters of 40–100 each. The eggs may float as a surface film but more often adhere to surface or subsurface vegetation.

**Similar species:** The squirrel treefrog is smaller, has a blunter nose, and lacks a distinct white lateral stripe. Pine Barrens treefrogs have a plum-colored stripe bordered dorsally with a narrow light line. Barking treefrogs are larger and often patterned dorsally with light ovals or ocelli.

**Comments:** Green treefrogs hybridize with barking treefrogs rather frequently and more rarely with Pine Barrens treefrogs. The appearance of such hybrids may be quite similar to a parent (apparently, most often the barking treefrog) or noticeably intermediate. The calls of the hybrids, however, are usually distinctive.

# 14. Pine Woods Treefrog

*Hyla femoralis*

**Size:** This is one of the smaller of Florida's treefrogs. A slender frog, the pine woods treefrog is adult at 1¼–1½ inches SVL. Females are the larger sex and may occasionally attain a length of 1¾ inches.

**Identification:** Pine woods treefrogs are variable and may be difficult to identify. Although the frog is most often reddish in color, gray and grayish green may also be assumed. A large dorsal figure of irregular shape is usually visible as is a dark lateral line that begins at the nostril, passes through the eye, curves downward posterior to the tympanum, and continues to the groin. A dark interorbital blotch is also usually discernible. The most distinctive markings are the light (often yellowish, sometimes greenish) irregularly oval spots on the dark concealed surface of the thigh.

Males have a dark throat and a rounded subgular vocal sac.

Tadpoles are olive to olive drab dorsally, purplish ventrolaterally, and yellowish ventrally.

**Voice:** Pine woods treefrogs have a curious and characteristic dot-dash call often likened to the sounds produced by Morse code transmissions. The call is rapidly paced at the breeding ponds, but slower when given as a treetop rain call. At some breeding ponds, calling males sit at night on open muddy shores; in other locations they may vocalize while sitting 1–7 feet above the water on the leaves of shoreline shrubs or the trunks of shoreline pines. They are rather easily approached on overcast or rainy nights but are much more wary on brilliantly moonlit nights. In the southern portion of the range the breeding calls may be heard as early as late February. In other areas they are more commonly heard from April to early October.

**Habitat/Range:** The common name pretty well defines the habitat where this frog is most commonly seen; however, it may also be encountered amid cypress trees, near and on dwellings, and it is a common breeder in roadside ditches that are near pinelands. In Florida this species is absent only from the Everglades.

**Abundance:** This is another of Florida's common to abundant treefrog species.

**Behavior:** Like many other treefrogs, the pine woods treefrog is strongly arboreal. It is seldom seen except when calling at the breeding ponds. Rain calls may be voiced from treetop positions.

**Reproduction:** Clusters of 20–100 eggs are laid until the total complement of several hundred is deposited. The eggs may float freely but more often adhere loosely to surface and subsurface vegetation. Ephemeral ponds are often chosen as breeding sites.

**Similar species:** The oval yellowish to greenish thigh spots are diagnostic but nearly impossible to see unless the treefrog is in hand.

**Comments:** This species is known to hybridize with both the Pine Barrens and gray treefrogs. Visually, the hybrids may be difficult to differentiate from the parent species, but the calls are often intermediate.

## 15. Barking Treefrog

*Hyla gratiosa*

**Size:** Although many are adult at 2 inches SVL, a record size of 2¾ inches has been confirmed. Females of this chunky treefrog are the larger sex.

**Identification:** Barkers are truly the chameleons of treefrogdom. The same frog may be yellowish green, green, tan, or brown, and may be patternless at one time and profusely marked with solid rounded spots or open-centered ocelli at another. Males have a greenish or yellow throat and a huge, rounded subgular vocal sac. The upper lip is white, and an irregular white lateral line may be present. The skin is strongly granular.

The tadpoles are often yellowish green dorsally and pinkish ventrally with a very high tail fin. A light line may run from the tail musculature to the eye, and a dark elongate marking may saddle the tail musculature somewhat anterior to midtail. Both the stripes and the dark saddle may be absent.

**Voice:** The barking treefrog has two distinctly different calls. A loud, oft repeated, but hollow-sounding "dooonk" is voiced when the frogs are floating in the breeding ponds, whereas the treetop rain call sounds more like a barking dog.

Barking treefrogs often call in conjunction with several other hylids but seem most often associated with choruses of green treefrogs. Hybridization with the green treefrog is well documented.

**Habitat/Range:** Barking treefrogs are found throughout Florida except for the Everglades and the southernmost tip of the state. This frog is associated with pinelands, open mixed woodlands, farmlands, and pasture ponds. It climbs high and well, apparently foraging both while high in trees and when closer to the ground. Winter congregations of a dozen or more dormant individuals have been found in sandy soils at the bases of fallen pines and pine stumps as well as beneath bark shards fallen from a long-dead but still-standing pines and oaks. These frogs call on warm nights while floating in rather open, shallow waters, often in pasture or open woodland ponds. More rarely, they call while low on pondside trees.

**Abundance:** This, our largest native eastern treefrog, remains common in some areas but may be reduced in numbers where habitat alterations have occurred or where it is collected heavily for the pet trade.

**Behavior:** Males often float while vocalizing and retain their calling position by grasping the stems of emergent vegetation or water surface plants with their fingers.

Barking treefrogs hybridize with green treefrogs in both altered and natural habitats.

In some cases male green treefrogs have been seen intercepting and amplexing female barking treefrogs. In other cases male barkers floating near the edges of ponds have intercepted female green treefrogs responding to calling males of their own species.

**Reproduction:** The 500 to more than 1,000 eggs may be deposited either singly or in sizable clusters and adhere to submerged or pond-bottom vegetation. Drawn to ponds by warm, heavy rains, barking treefrogs may be heard from early February to September.

**Similar species:** When present, the dorsal ocelli are diagnostic.

**Comments:** Even on overcast or rainy nights, barking treefrogs may be wary. Floating frogs will dive quickly if disturbed by ripples. They seldom resume calling at the site where they were frightened, surfacing, instead, several feet away.

# 16. Squirrel Treefrog

*Hyla squirella*

**Size:** This is a rather small and slender treefrog. Adult males may measure slightly less than 1 inch, while occasional large females may measure 1⅝ inch.

**Identification:** Squirrel treefrogs are both variable and rather nondescript. They change colors rapidly, varying between brown, yellow green, and bright green as well as all shades between these colors. The back and sides may be either unicolored or have darker smudges or blotches. Squirrel treefrogs often have a light upper lip and may have a vaguely defined light or dark lateral line. An interorbital blotch, spot, or triangle and darker orbital stripes may be present.

Males have a rounded subgular vocal sac.

The tadpoles are olive green dorsally and have a dark-centered yellow(ish) venter. The gills may show through the translucent skin with a reddish blush.

**Voice:** The common name refers to the rapidly repeated churring rain call voiced from trees, shrubs, logs, and stumps during periods of unsettled weather. The breeding call has a somewhat slower pulse rate, is more slowly repeated, and is more reminiscent of a duck's quack.

**Habitat/Range:** This ubiquitous treefrog is found throughout Florida including the Keys. It utilizes all manner of habitats, from open woodlands and cypress heads to pasturelands, gardens, and dwelling walls.

**Abundance:** The squirrel treefrog is an abundant species.

**Behavior:** Although squirrel treefrogs can be alert and agile, they often allow close approach without taking fright. This is especially true on cloudy or rainy nights at breeding ponds and puddles. They are agile climbers but also seek refuge in moisture-retaining natural and man-made ground debris.

**Reproduction:** This is a fecund species. Females may lay more than 800 eggs. The eggs may be deposited singly or in clusters. Breeding takes place in woodland or pasture ponds, flooded roadside ditches, or other suitable bodies of water. Males call while sitting on muddy shorelines or, more often, while hunkered down amidst low grasses in only an inch or two of water. Breeding activities begin at different times at different latitudes on the peninsula but usually coincide with the onset of spring and summer rains; however, squirrel treefrogs are known to breed from late February into the months of summer.

**Similar species:** The squirrel treefrog is best identified by assessing its negative characteristics. The squirrel tree frog has a rounder nose and less well-defined lateral stripe than the green treefrog. The squirrel treefrog lacks orange or yellow in the groin, and it lacks light spotting on the concealed surfaces of the thighs.

One positive is the presence of well-developed toe pads. These are lacking in the cricket frogs and poorly developed in the chorus frogs.

**Comments:** This is a frog you may need to catch to positively identify. Consider all negative field characters together and rule out the impossibilities.

# 17. Cuban Treefrog

*Osteopilus septentrionalis*

**Size:** This is the largest firmly established non-native treefrog in Florida. Males are adult at 1½–2¾ inches. Females regularly exceed a 3-inch SVL and occasionally exceeds a heavy-bodied 5¼ inches.

**Identification:** The ground color of the Cuban treefrog varies from tan or gray, through warm brown, to an olive (rarely bluish) green. A dorsal pattern may or may not be visible. The frog may be very light at night or when resting on a light-colored surface (such as a white wall). The dorsum is warty. The toe pads are proportionately immense. Yellow is often present in the axil of each foreleg. The venter is white or off-white. The dorsal and lateral surfaces are variably patterned.

The tadpoles are nearly black dorsally with a lighter venter. The tail musculature may have a brownish tinge.

When inflated, the bilateral vocal sacs make the male Cuban treefrog appear to be wearing water wings.

**Voice:** Variable. Vocalizing males produce snoring sounds interspersed with notes comparable to wet fingers being drawn over an inflated balloon.

**Habitat/Range:** In Florida this West Indian frog is often associated with man, but also occurs in tropical hammocks on the southern mainland and throughout the Keys. It is found in garden settings, among irrigated shrubs, along periodically flooded drainage ditches and other such artificial/modified habitats. By day and in dry weather this primarily nocturnal frog may secrete itself in open pipes, the axils of banana "trees," palms and other moisture retaining areas.

**Abundance:** Common to abundant in urban and suburban settings from Pinellas County on the west coast to Alachua County in north central Florida and Duval County on the east coast, southward through the Florida Keys. Populations are now present in Nassau, Marion, and Alachua counties and a few individuals have been found in Leon County.

**Behavior:** Cuban treefrogs usually allow close approach, but if startled are capable of making tremendous leaps. Although they are occasionally encountered on the ground or beneath debris, Cuban treefrogs are highly arboreal and the large toe pads enable them to assume and retain positions that would be otherwise precarious. Males may call from the tops of citrus or other such trees during rainstorms. The rain call is shorter and less varied than the breeding vocalizations.

**Reproduction:** This frog may breed anytime from March throughout the months of summer in the Keys but is more apt to breed between mid-April and August, after warm weather has truly set in, on the mainland. Clusters of 25 to 75 floating eggs are laid. A total complement of more than 300 may be laid.

**Similar species:** Both the pine woods and Cope's gray treefrogs have a white suborbital spot. No other treefrog in Florida has the proportionately immense toe pads of the Cuban.

**Comments:** The Cuban treefrog continues to expand its range northward. It is still killed in immense numbers by the occasional freezes, but enough obviously survive to quickly repopulate an area. Males seem to live only one or two years (researcher Walter Meshaka considers males "annuals" [pers. comm.]), but females may survive more than a decade.

Despite the toxicity of the skin secretions, Cuban treefrogs are preyed on by many Florida snakes. Alligators, turtles, raccoons, opossums, and birds of prey also eat these frogs.

**Caution:** The skin secretions of the Cuban treefrog are highly irritating to mucous membranes (eyes, nose, and mouth). Wash your hands *thoroughly* after handling this species.

## 18. Australian Great Green Treefrog

*Pelodryas caerulea*

**Comments:** If truly established in Florida, this magnificent jade green to olive-brown treefrog remains rare and localized in distribution. The Lee and Collier county populations of the 1990s are apparently extirpated but this treefrog has more recently been reported from Broward County. It seems to be a habitat generalist. Usually adult at 2 ½ to 3 inches SVL, occasionally examples may near or slightly exceed a 5 inch SVL. The calls are hoarse croaks. We provide a photograph for the purpose of identification.

### Chorus Frogs: Genus *Pseudacris*

This group of small hylid frogs contains Florida's smallest species, the little grass frog. It is adult at a slender ⅝ inch in length. Even the largest Florida chorus frog, the ornate, attains an average SVL of only 1¼ inches.

The toe pads of chorus frogs are relatively tiny. The frogs are usually encountered in terrestrial situations, but the spring peeper readily climbs when the opportunity presents itself. Preferring a cool weather breeding season, Florida's chorus frogs utilize shallow ephemeral ponds, puddles, and ditches during the months of winter and spring to vocalize and breed. They may be heard by day (especially on overcast days) or night. These are well-camouflaged, secretive frogs that can be difficult to locate.

# 19. Northern Spring Peeper

*Pseudacris crucifer crucifer*

Northern
Southern

**Size:** This small but attractive treefrog is adult at between ¾ and 1¼ inches in length. The females are larger and more robust than the males.
**Identification:** Color is variable, but to a lesser degree than that of many hylids. The dorsal ground color may be tan, russet, or some shade of brown to brownish gray. Some peepers seem vaguely suffused with olive. Cold or stressed frogs are darkest. A dark X is usually discernible on the dorsum. The sides of the snout are often darker than the top, and a dark lateral stripe is often present on each side. Males have a yellowish to grayish chin and a single subgular vocal sac. This race usually has little, if any, black pigmentation on the grayish white belly.

The tadpole is quite nondescript. The body, which is darkest dorsally, is greenish with vague stipplings or reticulations. The tail musculature and finnage are the same color as the body but may be more strongly patterned.
**Voice:** The vocalizations of this small hylid are probably recognized by more persons than those of any other eastern North American frog. The calls, strident whistled peeps with a rising inflection, are produced in series. The calls are most slowly given on cold nights. Peepers may produce occasional short trilling territorial calls. Once choruses are in full swing, peepers may call even on moonlit nights when temperatures dip into the low 40s; however, at such cold temperatures the little frogs frighten easily and may not resume calling once disturbed.
**Habitat/Range:** Peepers are frogs of open woodland and woodland ponds, of marshes and bogs. Although their breeding biology is rather well understood, little is known about their life away from the breeding ponds. Peepers have been occasionally found in the summer months

sitting on the leaves of low herbs such as trillium and jack-in-the-pulpit. This peeper ranges westward from Florida's Apalachicola River valley throughout the panhandle and is common throughout much of the eastern United States and southeastern Canada.

**Abundance:** The northern spring peeper is abundant throughout its range but seldom seen after the breeding season.

**Behavior:** Much about the life of the spring peeper remains a mystery. Its natural history is badly in need of study.

**Reproduction:** In Florida the spring peeper—a harbinger of impending northern spring weather—would be better referred to as a winter peeper. These little frogs begin vocalizing after cool weather has begun (usually during the rains of late November or early December) and may be heard at the ponds throughout the winter until shortly after the warm days of spring have set in. Males may choose to seclude themselves in a clump of grass when calling or be completely exposed on a patch of mud or a low branch. The eggs, which may near or slightly exceed 200 in number, are laid singly or in small clusters. They adhere to submerged vegetation.

**Similar species:** The pine woods treefrog has yellow to greenish oval spots on the rear surface of each thigh. When brown, the squirrel treefrog can be very similar to peepers in appearance; however, squirrel treefrogs lack the dark dorsal X. Other small chorus frogs tend to have dorsal markings in the form of stripes and a white(ish) lip.

**Comments:** The spring peeper was long considered a member of the genus *Hyla*, the "true" treefrogs. Although it has been relegated to the current genus, it does not fit well here. It has been suggested by some researchers that the peeper differs sufficiently from both the treefrogs and the chorus frogs to warrant the erection of a new genus.

20. Southern Spring Peeper, *Pseudacris crucifer bartramiana*, is common on the northern two-fifths of the Florida peninsula and the eastern half of the panhandle. The dorsum is often a rather pale tan and the dark X poorly defined. The light-colored venter is variably pigmented with black spots and stippling.

# 21. Upland Chorus Frog

*Pseudacris feriarum*

**Size:** The record size for a female (the larger sex) of this slender frog is 1½ inches. .

**Identification:** Light to dark brown is the most commonly seen ground color. As with most frogs, the colors are the lightest during periods of activity and darkest when the frogs are cold or inactive. The lateral stripes are the most prominent and usually not broken. The dark brown vertebral and dorsolateral stripes are relatively narrow and often broken into elongate spots. The dorsolateral stripes may be more prominent than the vertebral stripe. A dark interorbital triangle is usually visible. The venter is light but may bear dark pepper spots anteriorly. Males have a dark throat and rounded subgular vocal sac.

The tadpoles are very dark dorsally, gold ventrally, and the tail is dark tipped.

**Voice:** This is another of the chorus frogs with a trilling "combtooth" voice. When compared at similar temperatures the pulse rate of the trills is usually more rapid and of a higher pitch than the vocalizations of the more widespread southern chorus frog, but the two calls can be difficult to differentiate.

Males usually vocalize from amidst emergent grasses but may occasionally sit on open mud banks while calling.

**Habitat/Range:** In Florida, the upland chorus frog is a floodplain and low woodland species. It breeds in marshes, swamps, and temporarily flooded areas. In Florida it occurs in only a few of the panhandle counties from the Apalachicola drainage westward.

**Abundance:** This frog is of localized distribution but not rare in Florida.

**Behavior:** Very little is known about the behavior of this winter breeding frog in Florida.

**Reproduction:** The several hundred eggs are laid in small clusters that adhere to subsurface vegetation and twigs.

**Similar species:** Spring peepers have a dark X on the back. Cricket frogs have fully webbed rear feet and stripes on the rear surface of the thighs. Southern and Florida chorus frogs are usually gray with black markings.
**Comments:** North of Florida this species is associated with upland habitats.

# 22. Southern Chorus Frog

*Pseudacris nigrita nigrita*

☐ Southern
■ Florida

**Size:** This hylid frog is adult at a slender 1 inch in length. Occasional females may attain 1¼ inches SVL.
**Identification:** This is a light tan, grayish tan, or russet frog with a prominent dark (often black) lateral stripe and three rows of dorsal stripes or blotches (also often black). The ground color is darkest when the frog is cold and undisturbed. The upper lip of the southern chorus frog is usually an unbroken white and precisely delineated dorsally. The venter is light. Males have a dark throat that distends into a large subgular vocal sac.

The small tadpoles are dark with yellowish or golden flecks.
**Voice:** Although the trill rate varies with temperature (being slower when cold), the voice of this frog is best described as the noise made when a fingernail is drawn over the teeth of a pocket comb.
**Habitat/Range:** These tiny, agile, and seldom seen frogs call from flooded fields, rain-swollen marshes, drainage ditches, pine woodland ponds, and other such open habitats. They are also associated with ponds and flooded shallows in woodlands with thick herbaceous understories. The southern chorus frog occurs on the northwestern one-fifth of the peninsula and throughout the panhandle.
**Abundance:** Because of its secretive nature, population statistics for this frog are difficult to ascertain. In recent years we have found this species rare or absent in many Florida locations where it was once common, but still abundant in others. Where ephemeral wetlands have been modified

or eliminated, the frogs are notably absent, yet they may occasionally be common in roadside ditches in populated areas.

**Behavior:** When calling, Florida chorus frogs are usually well concealed amidst fallen limbs or emergent grasses. Often only their heads or head and anterior bodies are above the water surface.

**Reproduction:** Although these frogs are often spoken of as winter breeders, in Florida the breeding time is dictated by the occurrence of rains and may extend well into the warmer months. The up to several hundred eggs are laid in loose clusters and attached to submerged twigs and vegetation.

**Similar species:** Cricket frogs have extensive webbing on their hind feet and distinct stripes on the rears of the thighs. The dorsal markings of the brownish tan upland chorus frog are usually a deeper brown, not black, and the white lip stripe may not be as precisely delineated dorsally.

23. Florida Chorus Frog, *Pseudacris nigrita verrucosa,* is the southern representative of this species. It may be heard calling from pinewoods ponds, flooded pasture depressions, and roadside ditches from Nassau County in the east and Dixie County in the west, southward through the peninsula. Many overlapping characteristics occur where the ranges of this subspecies and the more northerly southern chorus frog abut. Individual frogs can vary tremendously in color and intensity of pattern. Cold frogs can be so dark gray that the charcoal markings are barely discernible. When warm the same frog can display a ground color of the lightest gray and with boldly contrasting elongate spots of deep charcoal; even the lateral markings are in the form of elongate spots. Rarely the spots join to form stripes. Striping seems more common at the northern end of the range than in the south. The upper lip may be mostly white or mostly black but almost always has alternating patches of those colors; the lip is seldom solid white.

In more southerly areas of the state, winter rains may occur, but the rainy season is usually in the late spring to autumn. Therefore, rather than being exclusively a winter breeder as is often suggested, the Florida chorus frog may vocalize and breed at any time of year on the southern peninsula.

This frog is seldom seen once breeding has ceased for the year.

# 24. Little Grass Frog

*Pseudacris ocularis*

**Size:** Males of this diminutive frog—the smallest anuran of the United States—are slender and attain a SVL of only ½ inch. Occasional large females may attain a full ⅝ inch in length.

**Identification:** The ground color of this species is variable, but almost always light tan, rusty red, or dark brown. More rarely the frog may be suffused with olive. It is often brighter dorsally than laterally. A darker vertebral stripe and/or two dorsolateral stripes may be visible. A prominent dark lateral stripe begins at the tip of the snout and continues along each side to the groin. A dark interorbital triangle is usually visible. Little grass frogs are often most brightly colored during periods of daytime activity and are lightest and least contrastingly colored on warm nights. They are darkest when the weather (and the frog) are cold. The belly is light, often with a yellowish tint anteriorly. Males have a dark throat and proportionately huge subgular vocal sac.

The tadpole is olive dorsally and pinkish ventrally. The pinkish color or a yellowish suffusion extends onto the tail musculature. A dark line is usually present centrally on the tail musculature, and dark spots are present on the edges of the fins.

**Voice:** This tiny hylid is an opportunistic breeder, and its high-pitched tinkling calls may be heard for throughout most of the year.

**Habitat/Range:** This little chorus frog is a denizen of grassy pond and cypress bay margins, swamp and marsh edges, flooded meadows, grassy pasture ponds, and roadside drainage ditches. It is found throughout all of Florida save for the westernmost panhandle.

**Abundance:** This is an abundant species but difficult to observe.

**Behavior:** This frog may hop from grasses when startled but is usually not seen unless a concerted effort is made to find it. Even then it is easily overlooked. It is most easily seen as it calls at night in flooded roadside ditches. Look for it from just above water surface level to 3 feet above the water on emergent grasses.

**Reproduction:** Despite their small size, females of the little grass frog may lay more than 200 eggs. These are laid in several clusters of 25 or more attached to underwater twigs and grasses.

**Similar species:** Cricket frogs have more extensively webbed hind feet and stripes on the rear of the thighs. Other chorus frogs are larger, and most have a pattern of dorsal and dorsolateral spots that may be discrete or coalesced into rough-edged stripes.

**Comments:** When calling, this hylid often aligns itself with the stem on which it is sitting; its grass-hued ground color and striped pattern allow it to blend almost imperceptibly into its background. At other times, when the little grass frog positions itself across the stem, it becomes slightly more visible.

# 25. Ornate Chorus Frog

*Pseudacris ornata*

**Size:** This is the largest and most robust of Florida's chorus frogs. Males, the smaller sex, are adult at from 1 to 1¼ inches SVL. Occasional females may near 1½ inches.

**Identification:** This is the most variably colored of the chorus frogs. The ground color may vary from dull to bright green, be gray, brown, or russet, or be various combinations of these colors. A dark interorbital triangle is usually present. Broad dorsolateral stripes may be prominent or barely visible. Prominent light-edged black lateral markings are present. These consist of a stripe that begins on the tip of the snout and continues rearward to the tympanum or beyond, a side stripe or spot (this may coalesce with the eyestripe), and (usually) two vertically oriented elongate spots in the groin. The venter usually has a yellowish blush, strongest posteriorly, and brighter yellow spots beneath the hind legs. Males have a dark throat and a rounded subgular vocal sac.

The tadpoles are brownish dorsally and somewhat lighter ventrally. They have broad tail fins.

**Voice:** The metallic, abruptly ended peeps, voiced in series, are unlike the calls of any other Florida chorus frog.

**Habitat/Range:** Pine and mixed woodland ponds, seasonally flooded meadows, and roadside ditches are among the many habitats used. The ornate chorus frog once ranged in suitable habitat over the northern half of the peninsula and throughout the panhandle of Florida.

**Abundance:** Although still locally common in northern Florida and on the panhandle, more southern populations are diminished or extirpated.

**Behavior:** A persistent burrower, the ornate chorus frog is usually seen above ground only at breeding ponds or when foraging during rainy weather. Males may call while sitting exposed on mud banks, floating in open water, or from concealed locations in grasses on the shore or in very shallow water. Males often hold onto surface grasses or twigs with their fingers and vocalize while floating.

**Reproduction:** The more than 100 (probably to several hundred) eggs are laid in small clusters and attached to submerged twigs and vegetation.

**Similar species:** No other frog within the range of this species has similar bold black lateral spots.

**Comments:** This is the most distinctively marked of the eastern chorus frogs. The prominent black lateral markings make identification easy, no matter the dorsal color or pattern.

## NARROW-MOUTHED TOADS: FAMILY MICROHYLIDAE

The eastern narrow-mouthed toad is the only representative of this family in Florida. It is so rounded that its appearance has been likened to that of a marble with legs and a nose. Termites and ants seem the major food items of this frog. Narrow-mouths are so secretive that they can be present in large numbers but their presence not suspected.

Narrow-mouths run or make short erratic hops rather than graceful leaps.

## A Marble with a Mouth

Whether perceived as *peeeeeeeet*s or *baaaaaaaa*s, the vocalizations of eastern narrow-mouthed toads are often heard as the inch-long anurans plaintively bleat from freshly rain-filled roadside ditches or ephemeral ponds.

The narrow-mouthed toad (sometimes called a frog, but it actually makes no difference) is quite probably our most distinctive anuran. After all, how can you misidentify a toad that looks like a marble with a point in one end (its nose) and has somehow sprouted four tiny legs? You'd have to agree—that's distinctive!

In fact, when it's first seen, usually when accidentally uncovered when a fallen board, limb, or piece of debris is moved, until one sees its hopping escape-scuttle, this toad may be mistaken for a fallen acorn or sprouting dark-colored mushroom. And disbelief sets in when a person is first shown the marble-sized toad and told it is the producer of the loud bleating—almost overpowering in chorus—coming from the newly formed puddles in his or her yard.

I'm no longer particularly surprised by anything I see or hear about narrow-mouths. I might find one beneath debris on a bed of nearly dry sand so hot it is uncomfortable to touch. A specimen might be found hunkered down quietly amidst seething ants beneath a sheet of tin. After a seeming absence of 15 years, one turned up in our highway-surrounded neighborhood this past summer.

Where the species is common, any puddle-making rainstorm can bring a sufficient number together to create a deafening chorus for nights on end.

In short, these are amazingly resilient, wonderfully intriguing, unmistakable little anurans!

# 26. Eastern Narrow-mouthed Toad

*Gastrophryne carolinensis*

**Size:** Males are adult at an inch or less in length. Occasional females slightly exceed 1¼ inches.

**Identification:** Narrow-mouthed toads are often darker dorsally than laterally. The back varies from charcoal to olive brown, russet, or bluish gray. A dorsal pattern of darker reticulations or a broad, dark-edged brown, russet, or terra cotta dorsal figure is often present. The lower sides and venter are heavily pigmented gray or olive brown. Males have a darker throat. A fold of skin crosses the back of the head just posterior of the eyes. This little toad is ovoid when viewed from above and has short, heavy legs.

The single subgular vocal sac is round.

The black tadpoles are flecked with slate blue and may have a tan lateral line. When viewed in profile, the anterior venter slopes sharply upward into a pointed head. The tail fins are dark flecked and dark tipped.

**Voice:** The call of the male is a penetrating, sheeplike bleat.

**Habitat/Range:** Eastern narrow-mouthed toads are found in a wide variety of habitats from urban lots to woodlands and sandy pinelands. Where drainage is sharp, these toads are most common near the environs of ponds, lakes, swamps, and marshes. They persist in suburban lawns and may be especially abundant in sandy soils where lawns and gardens are sprinkled daily. Narrow-mouths are accomplished burrowers and seldom seen on the surface of the ground. They may be found beneath boards, rocks, leaf litter (including mats of pine needles), and other moisture-retaining debris.

**Abundance:** The narrow-mouth is often present in many urban and suburban habitats, but despite being common, it is a secretive and seldom-seen frog. It is known from every county in the state.

**Behavior:** This little burrower is primarily nocturnal. It is drawn to the breeding ponds by heavy spring and early summer rains. Sticky skin secretions assist amplexing males in retaining their position.

**Reproduction:** These little toads may breed in situations as ephemeral as shallow drainage ditches or in places where water is more permanent. They may be particularly common in the shallows of grassy, semipermanent ponds and irrigated agricultural areas. Narrow-mouths often call while hunkered down amidst water-edge or emergent grasses and when so positioned are difficult to see. Occasionally they may call while floating or while sitting exposed on a bank. The floating eggs are deposited in small clusters. A total of more than 800 eggs has been recorded from a single female. Amplexus is axillary (behind the forelimbs).

**Similar species:** None. No other anuran in Florida has a pointed head with a skin-fold behind the eyes.

**Comments:** Males have been observed calling on rainy nights while buried in damp sand with only head and vocal sac exposed.

## TRUE FROGS: FAMILY RANIDAE

**Taxonomic note:** It has recently been suggested that the generic name of eastern frogs be changed from *Rana* to *Lithobates*. The proposed change remains controversial, so we have elected to retain usage of the long-used name *Rana* in this volume.

The ranids are the typical, long-legged, long-leaping frogs that are, with one exception in Florida (the gopher frog), associated with damp meadows and lakes, ponds, rivers, ditches, and other moist or wet habitats. Most Florida species have extensive webbing between the toes and web-free fingers. None in Florida have toe pads.

Breeding is often initiated by rains but may occur spontaneously in dry weather if all other conditions are suitable.

Although many species are warm-weather breeders, others breed while water temperatures are still cold during the short days and long nights of winter. The tympani (exposed eardrums) of adult males of the bull, bronze, pig, river, and carpenter frogs are conspicuously larger than the eye. The tympani of adult females of these five species are about the size of the eye. Despite the Florida bog frog being closely allied to the bronze frog, the tympani of adult males of the bog frog are only marginally larger proportionately than those of the adult females.

The tympani of both sexes of the pickerel, southern leopard, and the subspecies of the gopher frog are similarly sized.

Adult males of some species (bull and bronze frogs) have yellow throats.

The arms and thumb-bases of all reproductively active male ranids are enlarged.

Vocal sac morphology varies in Florida ranids. It is bilateral and internal, single and internal (both causing the vocalizing male to look as though it has mumps) on some species, or bilateral and external (like water wings) on others.

The skin is usually relatively smooth, but may bear tubercles or glandular (dorsolateral) ridges. The presence or lack of dorsolateral ridges will need to be considered in species identifications.

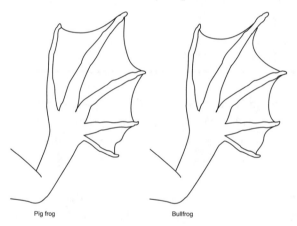

Pig frog          Bullfrog

## 27. Florida Gopher Frog

*Rana capito aesopus*

**Taxonomic note:** Some authorities have suggested that *R. capito* is merely variable in color and that no subspecific designations are warranted.
**Size:** Although usually smaller, Florida gopher frogs occasionally attain a length of slightly more than 4 inches.

**Identification:** The Florida gopher frog has a ground color of grayish white to a rather dark gray, rarely with purplish overtones. Cold frogs are often so dark that the markings are all but obscured. Dark, rather well-defined horizontally elongated spots with irregular edges are present dorsally. The dorsal spots may be vaguely outlined with a lighter pigment. The lateral spots of more irregular shape are also present but may be more poorly defined. A prominent orange or yellow (males) or yellow to dark (females) dorsolateral ridge is present. Some yellow may be present in the axillae and groin. A similarly colored but often less prominently delineated, lateral ridge runs along the lip, above the forelimb to the groin. The venter may be light and basically unmarked (east and south) or rather dark and blotched (western panhandle).

The Florida gopher frog is comparatively short bodied and stubby and has a proportionately large head.

Males have huge bilateral vocal sacs.

The tadpoles are greenish, lighter cranially with dark supraorbital spots. The upper tail fin is profusely spotted. The tail tip may be dark.

**Voice:** Males produce a loud, protracted, roaring snore.

**Habitat/Range:** Unlike most frogs associated with wet areas, the Florida gopher frog is a denizen of sandy scrub areas that also support the most viable colonies of gopher tortoises. When not in the ephemeral ponds that it prefers for breeding activities, the gopher frog often seeks refuge in the burrows of the gopher tortoise. More rarely the gopher frog may be associated with stump holes, rodent burrows, and ground debris. It is found throughout the panhandle and the northern two-thirds of the peninsula.

**Abundance:** The Florida gopher frog can be fairly common locally but is a seldom-seen, secretive habitat specialist. Once found over most of peninsular Florida, it has become less common in recent years. Thorough population studies are needed to determine the actual remaining numbers of this frog.

**Behavior:** Following their breeding activities, Florida gopher frogs may disperse for long distances. Unlike most other frogs (except the strongly predatory bullfrog), gopher frogs readily consume smaller frogs (including others of their own species) and toads. The more standard frog fare of insects is also eaten.

**Reproduction:** Breeding activities by this frog are usually associated with heavy rains. In many cases, these rains refill breeding ponds that have been dry, or nearly dry, through seasonal nonrainy months. Gopher frogs are among the frogs to breed earliest in the year. Sizable choruses assemble at suitable ponds during heavy rains of February, March, and April. Males call while floating, often in water several feet in depth. The egg masses are attached to vegetation and may contain several thousand eggs.

**Similar species:** Leopard frogs are proportionately slender and have oval spots and a ground color of green, tan, or brown (or combinations of all). Their slenderness alone should differentiate leopard frogs from the stocky gopher frog. Pickerel frogs have bright yellow in the groin and squared dorsal spots.

**Comments:** The gopher frogs on Florida's western panhandle were once designated the Dusky Gopher Frog, *R. c. sevosa.*

However, genetic assessment has elevated the dusky gopher frog to a full species, *Rana sevosa* (27A), and it is now restricted in range to southeastern Mississippi; therefore the gopher frog of Florida's western panhandle has reverted to *R. c. aesopus.*

# 28. Bullfrog

*Rana catesbeiana*

**Size:** Although sexes are of nearly equal size, females are slightly larger. The record size of this, North America's largest frog, is 8 inches. A snout-vent-length of 4–6½ inches is more common.

**Identification:** Although bullfrogs are of some shade of green, some specimens may be so dark or heavily mottled or reticulated with darker pigment that they look almost black. The sides of the face and lips are usually the brightest green. The forelimbs may have dark spots, and the hind legs may be prominently banded with darker pigment. Males often have yellow throats. Females have white throats. The light venter may or may not be heavily pigmented. A prominent skin ridge extends back from the rear of the eye around the back of the tympanum and terminates above the foreleg. The last joint of the longest toe is devoid of webbing.

Despite the vocal sac being internal, the throat swells noticeably during vocalizations.

The tadpoles are olive (lighter ventrally), appear stippled, and have well-developed lateral lines.

**Voice:** The easily recognized voice of this species is a far-carrying, two- or three-syllabled "brrr-ummmmm" or "jug-o-rum." The largest male bullfrogs have the deepest voices.

**Habitat/Range:** Ponds, lakes, large ditches, canals, slow rivers and their oxbows are all suitable habitats for this frog. Immature bullfrogs often sit on the shore or in shallow water near the shore, but adults often frequent deeper water well away from shore. Adults may sit on or float among lily pads or other surface vegetation. Bullfrogs are found from Collier and Palm Beach counties northward through the peninsula and panhandle.

**Abundance:** This highly adaptive aquatic frog may be rather uncommon in the southern parts of its range but quite common in north Florida and on the panhandle. Metamorphs and juveniles are seen more frequently than the adults.

**Behavior:** Large, predatory, solitary (even intraspecifically confrontational during the breeding season, when males avidly battle other males) describe the behavior of the bullfrog. Bullfrogs are usually wary by day but rather easily approached at night. However, those floating are easily "spooked" by water ripples. Approach them carefully. Frightened bullfrogs may produce a single high-pitched note as they leap to safety or a loud scream if caught by a predator (including a human).

**Reproduction:** Huge rafts of from several thousand to about 20,000 floating eggs are produced. These hatch in several days, and prior to metamorphosis the tadpoles may attain a length of more than 3 inches. Although in the north metamorphosis can take two years or longer, in the comparatively warm waters of Florida, bullfrog tadpoles may metamorphose in just several months. Male bullfrogs may vocalize from pondside positions but are more often heard as they sit on floating debris or mats of vegetation or float on the water surface, often while among lily pads or other floating plants.

**Similar species:** Bullfrogs have a rather broadly rounded snout (when viewed from above). Pig frogs have a more sharply pointed snout, are heavily pigmented under the hind legs, and have fully webbed hind feet. River frogs have dark spots on the upper lip, white spots on the lower lip, and a heavily pigmented, dark throat and belly. Bronze frogs have dorsolateral ridges.

**Comments:** This huge frog, once a staple of frog's legs, is still hunted for food, the pet trade, and biological studies throughout much of its range. Bullfrogs seem to be slowly expanding their range southward on the Florida peninsula. Common throughout the eastern and central United States, bullfrogs, probably intended as a food source, have been introduced to our western and pacific states as well as elsewhere in the world.

## 29. Bronze Frog

*Rana clamitans clamitans*

**Taxonomic note:** It has been recently suggested that rather than containing two subspecies, *Rana clamitans* can be divided into three full species. Until this is more widely accepted, we will retain the more standard nomenclature.

**Size:** Occasional adults may attain or slightly exceed 3 inches SVL.

**Identification:** More often than not, this small frog is an unrelieved bronzy brown dorsally and laterally, but it may occasionally be green. The snout and upper lips vary from a brown lighter than the body to a lime green. There are light and dark spots on the lower lip. A light stripe is often present beneath the eye. The belly is light (almost white) with profuse dark vermiculations. Metamorphs have a more strongly patterned venter than adults. Prominent "three-quarter length" dorsolateral ridges are present. The center of the tympanum (external eardrum) of the male is elevated.

The bilateral vocal pouches are internal. Both body and throat swell noticeably when the frog choruses. Adult males usually have a yellow throat.

Tadpoles are dark brownish green dorsally, light ventrally. The upper tail fin is prominently dark spotted, the lower is less so.

**Voice:** This is the "banjo-frog" of marshes, woodland streams, and ponds. The call notes, usually given while the frog sits in shallow water or concealed in water-edge vegetation, is a single strong "plunk." Several plunks of diminishing volume may follow. Both sexes produce a shrill scream when captured by a predator (including man), and a high-pitched cry of shorter duration is often given when a startled frog jumps into the water.

**Habitat/Range:** Streams and associated pools, river edges, and vegetated oxbows, ponds, and lakesides are all acceptable habitats to this adaptable frog. It often sits concealed in water-edge vegetation. It can be found in the northern two-fifths of peninsular Florida and throughout the panhandle.

**Abundance:** Bronze frogs may be common but are usually not really abundant. They can be uncommon at the southern extreme of their range.

**Behavior:** Bronze frogs are active by both day and night, They often sit in the patchy sunshine of water-edge grasses. When on the shore, these frogs leap quickly into the water when approached by day but are less easily startled at night. Males call while floating or while lying atop floating vegetation.

**Reproduction:** The surface film of one to several thousand eggs often adheres to emergent vegetation.

**Similar species:** Adults of the pig, river, and bull frogs are much larger, and all lack dorsolateral ridges. The bronze frog–sized carpenter frog (found in Florida only in Baker and Columbia counties) also lacks dorsolateral ridges. Southern leopard frogs have a sharper nose and are spotted. The Florida bog frog is smaller, may have prominent spots posteriolaterally, has reduced webbing on the hind feet, and is restricted to the panhandle counties of Okaloosa, Santa Rosa, and Walton.

**Comments:** These pretty little frogs are not extensively exploited commercially in Florida. The banjo-twang calls are enjoyable additions to quiet summer days at many favored fishing holes.

# 30. Pig Frog

*Rana grylio*

**Size:** Smaller and somewhat slimmer than the bullfrog, this frog, once referred to as the southern bullfrog, can attain nearly 6½ inches SVL. Most, though, are between 3½ and 5½ inches long. Males are usually notably smaller than females.

**Identification:** Adults of the pig frog vary in coloration from gray brown through olive brown to a pleasing rather bright green. Green specimens often have scattered large dark marks dorsally and laterally. The belly is light anteriorly but heavily vermiculated with dark pigment posteriorly. Juvenile pig frogs have light stripes on dark body and look superficially like carpenter frogs; however, the toes of the pig frog are webbed to the tips. Pig frogs lack dorsolateral ridges and have a sharply pointed snout.

Pig frogs have a single, broadly expanded internal vocal sac.

**Voice:** The common name says it all; the vocalizations may consist of only a single grunting call but are often voiced in series.

**Habitat/Range:** Pig frogs are generally distributed in most waterways, including rivers, streams, lakes, ponds, swamps, and marshes. They are highly aquatic (among the most aquatic of our frogs), and may either float in open water or choose a station on or amid floating or emergent vegetation. This species is found in every county in the state.

**Abundance:** This large frog does not seem as common now as in days gone by but may still be heard vocalizing on nearly any warm night.

**Behavior:** Despite its large size, pig frogs are easily startled. They are very difficult to approach by day, but at night, with a flashlight, are somewhat easier.

**Reproduction:** The more than 10,000 eggs are laid as a surface film. They may adhere to surface or emergent vegetation. Although pig frog tadpoles at the northern edge of the range reportedly take more than a year to metamorphose, those in the southern part of the range develop in considerably less time.

**Similar species:** The bullfrog has a blunter snout, can attain a greater size, has slightly less extensive webbing on the hind feet, and usually has a less pigmented belly. Adult carpenter frogs, which are quite similar in both dorsal and ventral colors to juvenile pig frogs, have less extensive webbing on the hind feet than that of the pig frog. Bronze frogs have dorsolateral ridges. Florida bog frogs (found only in the western panhandle) are very small and have reduced webbing on the hind feet. River frogs have dark and light spots on the lips.

**Comments:** Long a staple of the frog-leg industry, pig frogs are hunted and gigged at night from air- and John-boats. Many commercial hunters have recently indicated that pig frog populations currently seem diminished; however, it is known that populations of this frog are cyclic, declining in drought and erupting in wet years.

# 31. River Frog

*Rana heckscheri*

**Size:** With an occasional adult reaching 6¼ inches SVL, this is one of the three largest frogs in Florida. Most adults are fully grown at 4–5½ inches.

**Identification:** The river frog has a grayer and more rugose dorsum than the other large ranids with which it shares its habitat. The dorsal color varies between gray, grayish green, and brownish green. Poorly defined darker smudges are often present both dorsally and laterally. Light and dark spots present on the lips, and variably defined dark bars are on the hindlegs. The belly is gray with light markings. The throat may be darker than the belly. Males often have a yellow(ish) suffusion on the throat. There are no dorsolateral ridges. Webbing extends to the last phalanx of the longest toe.

The vocal sac is single and internal.

Tadpoles undergo ontogenetic color changes. Small tadpoles are very dark (often black) with a narrow but well-defined light ring around the body posterior to the eyes. With growth the ring obscures, the color lightens (at least somewhat), and the tail fin becomes edged with dark pigment.

**Voice:** Reproductively active males of this large frog make a deep, rolling, roaring snore. Shorter grunting calls are also emitted. The vocalizations of smaller river frogs are of a higher pitch than the sounds produced by large examples. Males call while sitting in shallow water or on the shore.

**Habitat/Range:** Despite the implications of its common name, the river frog may be found in and along lakes, ponds, swamps, and marshes as well as rivers. It often sits on the shore or on a floating log or other such vantage point. Populations are found from Hillsborough County on the Gulf coast and Volusia County on the Atlantic coast northward through the peninsula and panhandle.

**Abundance:** River frogs are typically quite common in suitable habitat; however, since 2005 it has seemed that I have found fewer than I would consider normal in previously heavily populated river frog habitats in north central Florida.

**Behavior:** This is a highly aquatic but often rather easily approached frog. This is especially so after dark with the help of a flashlight. River frogs often choose to sit and call from rather conspicuous stations along vegetation-free banks or from atop floating logs or other such solid debris. The tadpoles of this frog school, at times in vast numbers, and seem to show fidelity to certain areas in a body of water. Prior to metamorphosis they attain a length of more than 4 inches. When moving slowly the schools of tadpoles move in a rather synchronized manner; when disturbed they mill about. It is probable that schooling is an antipredator mechanism. In addition to the protection afforded by the noxious secretions in the skin of the large tadpoles, schooling indicates that there may well be safety in numbers.

**Reproduction:** The several thousand eggs are laid as a surface film, often among emergent vegetation to which they adhere. Tadpoles overwinter and take about a year to metamorphose.

**Similar species:** Bronze and Florida bog frogs are much smaller than adult river frogs, have dorsolateral ridges, and do not have heavily mottled gray bellies. Carpenter frogs are smaller and have four bronzy stripes. Pig and bullfrogs have no light spots on their lips.

**Comments:** Rather than struggling to escape when captured, the river frog goes entirely limp. The noxious skin secretions are odorous.

# 32. Florida Bog Frog

*Rana okaloosae*

**Size:** At an adult size of slightly less than 2 inches, the bog frog is the smallest of Florida's ranid frogs.

**Identification:** In appearance the Florida bog frog is very similar to the bronze frog. The dorsum varies from yellowish green to greenish brown or brown. The three-quarter-length dorsolateral ridges are often light in color. The light venter bears dark vermiculations. There may be light spots on the green jaw. The tympanum is brown and has no raised center. The webbing of the hind feet is very reduced. At least two phalanges of each of the four shortest toes and three phalanges of the longest toe extend beyond the webbing.

The vocal sac is single and internal.

The tadpole of the bog frog is slender and has an elongate tail. It is brown dorsally and darker with white spots ventrally. The sides and tail have many light spots.

**Voice:** The series of low-pitched single clucking calls has little carrying power. The calls slow noticeably toward the end of the series. Males call while sitting on mud banks, resting in shallow water, or sprawled atop floating vegetation.

**Habitat/Range:** This is a frog of slowly moving acidic seeps and stream backwaters. Black titi, Atlantic white cedar, and sphagnum moss are among the plants commonly associated with these habitats. This species is found only in Walton, Santa Rosa, and Okaloosa counties.

**Abundance:** This uncommon frog is found only in a few acidic streams in Florida's western panhandle.

**Behavior:** Because of its limited distribution, precise habitat requirements, and apparently low numbers, the life history of the bog frog is in need of extensive research.

**Reproduction:** The several hundred eggs are laid in a surface film.

## Bogs and Frogs and Attacking Vines

In the 1980s, Paul Moler, a nongame biologist for the then-Florida Fresh Water Fish and Game Commission, was driving a rural road near Eglin Air Force Base in Okaloosa County. He'd pulled over near a creek at dusk and turned off the engine in his truck. The usual evening chorus of katydids, cricket frogs, and bronze frogs had begun, but that night he heard another voice in the chorus, a voice Paul could not identify. (Herpetologists who work in the field, as Paul seemed to spend most of his waking hours, learn frog and toad calls the way you'd know your child's voice in the dark).

Paul got out of his truck, pulled on his hip boots, and approached the creek. Typical for frogs, the vocalizers stopped calling as Paul waded in. Paul waited until the calls began again and moved forward slowly. It took a few minutes, but soon he could see the frog—and it looked a bit different from the common, well-known bronze frog he was used to seeing. He captured the frog, took it back to Gainesville, and began the exacting process of identifying the frog. Was it—could it be—a new species?

It was new, and the bog frog, *Rana okaloosae*, named for its home county, was described in 1985.

Two years later, unable to resist seeing a new species, Dick and I were on the same roadway, by the same creek, listening as dark fell. Within a few minutes, we could hear the various calls beginning—some loud, some soft—and, yes, among them there was a much softer frog call, a hammering call that dropped off quickly with a few feet of distance, that neither of us recognized. There was only one frog call in Florida we didn't recognize. We were among the bog frogs.

The creek was broad at this point, filled with plant life, and water flow was slow. We entered the creek, Dick with camera in hand and I with only a flashlight. Dick waded slowly, trying to locate the caller. I went in a few feet and waited to see whether I was needed to spring onto something as it darted past. I threaded my way through slender willow trees and played my light on the surface of the creek. The droplets on the outstretched pads of dozens of tiny sundews winked back at me as the light moved. Submerged sphagnum moss stood out in sharp relief, each tendril looking soft and pliable and waving slightly. Fist-sized hummocks of floating plants dotted the surface of the water, and for a moment my entire world was confined to the brightly lit V of my flashlight's beam.

*continued*

Then a muffled splash and Dick's sharp outcry brought me back to reality. Head up, I looked in the direction I last saw him and asked, "What happened?" Sounding dignified yet outraged, Dick said, "I was attacked by an inch-diameter vine *loaded* with wicked thorns—*Smilax*—and my waders are filled with water!"

Relieved that he was okay, I discarded the flow chart in my head (alligator y/n; big alligator y/n; save Dick y/n). His voice continued, "But I got some photos—the bog frog is immortalized!"

Soaked and smiling, we waded to shore, clambered back into the car, and set out on our next adventure—a search for Pine Barrens treefrogs. The night was young yet.

**Similar species:** The bronze frog has more extensive webbing on the hind feet, and the center of the male's tympanum is elevated. Neither the bull nor the pig frog has dorsolateral ridges.

**Comments:** Little is known with absolute certainty about the natural history of this tiny Florida endemic. It seems uncommon in some of its very specialized habitats and potentially susceptible to population reduction in others. This species is fully protected in Florida.

## 33. Florida Leopard Frog
*Rana sphenocephala sphenocephala*

## 34. Southern Leopard Frog
*Rana sphenocephala utricularia*

Southern
Florida

**Note:** Combined, these two subspecies, which are almost impossible to differentiate in the field, are the most abundant ranids in Florida (also see Comments).

**Size:** Although the record size is 5 inches, most are adult at 2¼ to 3½ inches SVL.

**Identification:** These are the most variably colored of Florida's frogs. The ground color may be brown, green (on Big Pine Key, nearly black), or a combination of both. The rounded to oval dark spots may be profuse or sparse but are often more sparing on the sides than on the back. Usually both tympani have a light center. The rear limbs are usually prominently marked with light-edged, elongate dark spots. The snout is rather sharply pointed. The prominent dorsolateral ridges are light in color.

When inflated during vocalizations, the paired, bilateral vocal sacs of the male look like water wings. When deflated, the sacs of some males remain visible as skin folds at the angle of the gape. Those of other males (especially those from peninsular Florida) are not outwardly visible when deflated.

The tadpoles are dark olive green dorsally and lighter ventrally. Both upper and lower tail fins are spotted.

**Voice:** Variable; chuckles or chickenlike clucks are interspersed with sounds best described as those made when a wet finger is rubbhed over an inflated balloon. These leopard frogs may be heard most frequently during the winter and spring months, but may call occasionally during even the hottest summer weather.

**Habitat/Range:** Both of these leopard frogs may wander far from the water into damp pastures, fields, and sodlands but are more often found in the environs of ponds, lakes, flooded ditches, irrigation and drainage canals, stream and river edges, backyard goldfish pools, and virtually any other body of water. These are among the few frogs able to colonize brackish coastal waters.

The southern leopard frog occurs throughout the panhandle counties and the northern one-fifth of the peninsula. The Florida leopard frog ranges southward from the vicinity of Alachua County to the southernmost Keys.

**Abundance:** These are the most abundant frogs in Florida.

**Behavior:** Leopard frogs are active and alert. If approached when ashore, they make as many leaps away from the water as toward it, with each leap often in a different direction.

**Reproduction:** The egg-clump is often found adhering to surface or subsurface vegetation. More than 1,000 eggs have been recorded either in a mass or in several clumps. Males call while floating in quite shallow water, usually from amidst emergent grasses.

**Similar species:** Of Florida frogs, only the two leopard frogs, the gopher frog and the pickerel frog, are prominently spotted. (The pickerel frog is rare and known only from Escambia County in the westernmost panhandle. It has squared or rectangular spots and yellow in the groin.) The gopher frog is of stocky build and has spots of irregular shape. The spots of the leopard frogs are more rounded or oval.

**Comments:** Rather than *Rana sphenocephala*, these leopard frogs are occasionally referred to as *R. utricularia*.

Males of *R. s. utricularia* bear vestigial oviducts (impossible to determine except at dissection), and the deflated vocal sacs are visible as folds at the side of the lower jaw. This frog is found on the northern one-fifth of the peninsula and the panhandle.

Males of *Rana s. sphenocephala* lack vestigial oviducts. The deflated vocal sacs fold inward out of sight and are very difficult to see. This race ranges over the southern four-fifths of the peninsula southward to and including the Keys.

# 35. Carpenter Frog

*Rana virgatipes*

**Size:** This is one of the smallest of Florida's true frogs. An adult SVL of 2½ inches may be attained, but most examples are smaller.

**Identification:** Although this is a four-striped frog, its dorsum may be so dark that the two dorsolateral stripes are all but obscured. The ground color is a greenish (sphagnum moss) brown. The two dorsolateral stripes are tan to light brown. The two lateral stripes seem invariably better defined. They are light tan to off-white and separate the dark dorsum from the strongly vermiculated black on white venter. The throat is only weakly pigmented. Carpenter frogs lack dorsolateral ridges. The webbing does not extend to the tip of the longest toe.

Males have large, external, bilateral vocal sacs. When deflated, these remain visible as dark folds at the angle of the jaws.

Tadpoles are dark olive black overall, The tail fin is not strongly spotted, but the spots on the upper fin may coalesce into a vague stripe halfway between the top of the fin and the musculature.

**Voice:** The series of half-dozen (or so) two-syllabled clacking calls diminish in volume toward the end. The calls are usually likened to hammerings, hence the common name of this frog.

**Habitat/Range:** In Florida, this persistently aquatic frog is associated with acidic cypress and tupelo swamps. It seems most common where extensive mats of sphagnum moss grow. It often sits amid emergent grasses. Look for it only near the Florida-Georgia state line in Baker and Columbia counties.

**Abundance:** Because in Florida the carpenter frog is found largely in the remote southern drainages of Georgia's Okefenokee Swamp, it is not a frequently seen species.

**Behavior:** Carpenter frogs rest on sphagnum mats or floating debris. They often sit among emergent grasses, where they blend, almost imperceptibly, into their background. They call both while floating (often while grasping grass or a twig with their fingers) and while sitting atop floating sphagnum and other surface or subsurface vegetation.

**Reproduction:** The carpenter frog is a spring and summer breeder. From 300 to more than 700 eggs are laid in a floating mass that usually adheres to, or wraps partially around, emergent vegetation. In the north tadpoles overwinter before metamorphosing. It is not known how long development and metamorphosis take in Florida.

**Similar species:** Bronze frogs have dorsolateral ridges. Florida bog frogs are found only on Florida's western panhandle. Bullfrogs lack dorsolateral striping. Immature pig frogs often have dorsolateral striping, but the webbing of the hind foot extends to the tip of the longest toe.

**Comments:** This frog has proven uncommon and difficult to find in Florida. It is much more easily found north of the state line, where it occurs as far as the Pine Barrens of New Jersey.

## SPADEFOOTS: FAMILY SCAPHIOPODIDAE

This frog family is represented in the United States by only six species, and in Florida by only one. These are burrowing anurans often referred to as spadefoot toads. Indeed, these creatures look much like toads but are differentiated by such external features as indistinct or absent parotoid glands and a vertically elliptical (rather than horizontal) pupil. A single dark-edged digging spade is present (toads have two) on the heel of each foot.

The breeding embrace of these toads is inguinal—that is, amplexing males grasp the females around the waist rather than just posterior to the forelimbs. Spadefoots breed in ephemeral pools. Breeding activity is stimulated by heavy (read "torrential") rains. Tadpole development is rapid, and metamorphosis, if hastened by drying pools, can occur in a matter of only two weeks. If the pools are more stable, metamorphosis may take longer.

True toad          Spadefoot toad

### Ephemeral Burps, Bleeps, Moans, and Groans

Eerie moans, groans, and burps issued from a newly flooded roadside ditch in Alachua County. It was September, but after an abnormally dry summer, we had just experienced a toad-strangler of a rainstorm that had at least dampened the long dry bottoms of ephemeral ponds and flooded roadside depressions and ditches. About 3 inches of rain had fallen in less than an

*continued*

hour. It was the kind of localized storm that occurs so frequently in Florida. It had almost immediately induced anuran activity, but the water would soak quickly into the parched sandy soils or run into storm drains, again leaving many of the frogs, toads, and treefrogs high and dry.

But there was one group, the spadefoots, formerly of the family Pelobatidae but now in their own family, the Scaphiopodidae, that just might benefit from the just-fallen rain. Unlike other frogs still "thinking about" taking a chance in the flooded ditches, the spadefoots were already in place, most males were chorusing, and a few pairs were already in amplexus. When it comes to taking advantage of breeding opportunities, spadefoots, truly arid-adapted anurans, waste no time at all.

In fact, when hastened by falling water level in the breeding puddle, the entire breeding sequence, from rainfall to metamorphosis, can be completed in two to three weeks. Development may take twice that length of time if water levels are stable. Now that's adaptation!

We have spadefoots in our yard, but in the 15 years we've lived in Alachua County, I have heard breeding choruses only three times. They bred once in our yard in a very shallow puddle (they never should have used), and I helped them along by keeping a bit of water in the depression with the garden hose. Two other times they called from more distant locales, and although I never checked on the ponds, the presence of hundreds of tiny metamorphs in our yards and in neighbors' yards indicated that the spadefoots had chosen well.

Considering the current vagaries of our weather patterns and the concurrent breakdown in the sequential breeding activities of many of our native anurans, it is good to know that there is one species that is nearly always ready to take advantage of any substantial rains a frustrated and beleaguered Mother Nature sends our way.

# 36. Eastern Spadefoot

*Scaphiopus holbrookii*

**Size:** Large females occasionally attain a 2¾-inch SVL; however, males seldom exceed 2 inches, and most are smaller.

**Identification:** This is a brownish or olive brown toad with cream to yellow markings and sparse reddish tubercles. The dorsum usually bears a light (often cream, yellow, or greenish) lyre-shaped marking. The sides are lighter than the dorsum and may bear dark spots. The venter is white. The round parotoid glands are quite indistinct. Pupils are vertically elliptical, and a single sharp digging spade is present on each heel.

The white subgular vocal sac is large but somewhat flattened.

Tadpoles are usually brownish dorsally and laterally. The translucent belly skin is yellowish.

**Voice:** Although researchers have reported occasional muffled, moaning grunts produced by spadefoots still in their burrows, most often they call while floating. Each loud, moaning croak seems the result of a prodigious effort. As a male calls, the center of his back is bowed downward, and his head and throat are lifted almost clear of the water.

**Habitat/Range:** Eastern spadefoots occur in most peninsular counties and in all panhandle counties. In Florida the eastern spadefoot colonizes open woodlands and woodland edges with sandy or yielding soils. Spadefoots sometimes persist in suburban areas where the use of insecticides is not rampant. This anuran burrows deeply. It is capable of undergoing rather extended fasts and emerges from its burrow to feed at irregular intervals.

**Abundance:** Where present this is usually an abundant anuran.

**Behavior:** These nocturnal anurans are among the most secretive of Florida's tailless amphibia. Eastern spadefoots stay well under the soil surface at most times. Decreasing barometric pressure, especially when associated with a wet front, heavy thundershower, or tropical storm, may induce spadefoots to emerge from their burrows to forage or to breed.

**Reproduction:** Spadefoots breed explosively in temporary pools and ponds. Depending on rains, breeding (which is induced by torrential rains) may occur annually or only every several years. Breeding congregations may occur in nearly any month of the year. The 150 or more eggs are laid in strings or in many irregular elongated clusters. The eggs may hatch in less than two days, and tadpole development and metamorphosis are rapid. If hastened by receding water levels and deteriorating water quality, the complete process from deposition to metamorphosis can take less than two weeks.

**Similar species:** True toads have horizontal pupils, prominent parotoid glands, and two tubercles rather than a single spade on each heel.

**Comments:** This anuran is a toad in appearance but not in actuality. These intriguing creatures are present in numbers in some sandy areas but may be entirely absent from what appear to be similar habitats. Skin secretions, which smell vaguely like garlic, are distasteful and may cause allergic reactions in humans.

1. Fowler's toad,
*Bufo fowleri*

2. Cane toad,
*Bufo marinus*

3. Oak toad,
*Bufo quercicus*,
vocalizing

3a. Oak toad, *Bufo quercicus*

4. Southern toad, *Bufo terrestris*, vocalizing

4a. Southern toad, *Bufo terrestris*

4b. Southern toad, *Bufo terrestris*, defense posture

5. Coqui, *Eleutherodactylus coqui*, vocalizing

6. Greenhouse frog, *Eleutherodactylus planirostris*, striped phase

6a. Greenhouse frog, *Eleutherodactylus planirostris*, mottled phase

7. Northern cricket frog, *Acris crepitans*

8. Southern cricket frog, *Acris gryllus gryllus*

9. Florida cricket frog, *Acris gryllus dorsalis*

Florida cricket frog, *Acris gryllus dorsalis*, vocalizing

10. Pine Barrens treefrog, *Hyla andersonii*

10a. Pine Barrens treefrog, *Hyla andersonii*, vocalizing

11. Western bird-voiced treefrog, *Hyla avivoca avivoca* gray phase, vocalizing

11a. Western bird-voiced treefrog, *Hyla avivoca avivoca*

12. Cope's gray treefrog, *Hyla chrysoscelis*

12a. Cope's gray treefrog, *Hyla chrysoscelis*, vocalizing

13. Green treefrog, *Hyla cinerea*, vocalizing

13a. Green treefrog, *Hyla cinerea*, metamorph

14. Pine woods treefrog, *Hyla femoralis*

15. Barking treefrog, *Hyla gratiosa*, green phase

15a. Barking treefrog, *Hyla gratiosa*, vocalizing

15b. Hybrid barking treefrog × green treefrog, *Hyla gratiosa* × *H. cinerea*

16. Squirrel treefrog, *Hyla squirella*, vocalizing

16a. Squirrel treefrog, *Hyla squirella*

17. Cuban treefrog, *Osteopilus septentrionalis*, gray phase

17a. Cuban treefrog, *Osteopilus septentrionalis*, green phase

18. Australian great green treefrog, *Pelodryas caerulea*

19. Northern spring peeper, *Pseudacris crucifer crucifer*

20. Southern spring peeper, *Pseudacris crucifer*

21. Upland
chorus frog,
*Pseudacris
feriarum*

22. Southern
chorus frog,
*Pseudacris
nigrita nigrita*

22a. Southern
chorus frog,
*Pseudacris
nigrita
nigrita*, russet
coloration

23. Florida chorus frog, *Pseudacris nigrita verrucosa*

24. Least chorus frog, *Pseudacris ocularis*

25. Ornate chorus frog, *Pseudacris ornata*, green phase

25a. Ornate chorus frog, *Pseudacris ornata*, brown phase

26. Eastern narrow-mouthed toad, *Gastrophryne carolinensis*, striped phase

26a. Eastern narrow-mouthed toad, *Gastrophryne carolinensis*, mottled phase

27. Florida gopher frog, *Rana capito aesopus*

27a. Florida gopher frog, *Rana capito aesopus*, vocalizing

27A. Dusky gopher frog, *Rana sevosa*

28. Bullfrog,
*Rana
catesbeiana*

29. Bronze
frog, *Rana
clamitans
clamitans*

30. Pig frog,
*Rana grylio*

31. River frog, *Rana heckscheri*

31a. River frog, *Rana heckscheri*, tadople

32. Florida bog frog, *Rana okaloosae*

33. Florida
leopard
frog, *Rana
sphenocephala
sphenocephala*,
green phase

33a. Florida
leopard
frog, *Rana
sphenocephala
sphenocephala*,
Big Pine Key
black phase

34. Southern
leopard
frog, *Rana
sphenocephala
utricularia*

35. Carpenter frog, *Rana virgatipes*

36. Eastern spadefoot, *Scaphiopus holbrookii*

37. Reticulated flatwoods salamander, *Ambystoma bishopi*

38. Frosted
flatwoods
salamander,
*Ambystoma
cingulatum*,
adult

38a. Frosted
flatwoods
salamander,
*Ambystoma
cingulatum*,
larva

39. Marbled
salamander,
*Ambystoma
opacum*

40. Mole
salamander,
*Ambystoma
talpoideum*

41. Tiger
salamander,
*Ambystoma
tigrinum*

41a. Tiger
salamander,
*Ambystoma
tigrinum*

42. Two-toed
amphiuma,
*Amphiuma
means*, profile

42a. Two-toed
amphiuma,
*Amphiuma
means,*
aberrant color

43. One-toed
amphiuma,
*Amphiuma
pholeter*

44.
Apalachicola
dusky
salamander,
*Desmognathus
apalachicolae*

45. Southern dusky salamander, *Desmognatus auriculatus*, adult

45a. Southern dusky salamander, *Desmognatus auriculatus*, larva

46. Spotted dusky salamander, *Desmognathus conanti*

47. Seal salamander, *Desmognathus monticola*

48. Southern
two-lined
salamander,
*Eurycea
cirrigera*,
normal phase

48a. Southern
two-lined
salamander,
*Eurycea
cirrigera*,
bright-colored
sandhills male

49. Three-lined
salamander,
*Eurycea
guttolineata*

50. Dwarf
salamander,
*Eurycea
quadridigitata*

51. Georgia
blind
salamander,
*Haideotriton
wallacei*

52. Four-toed
salamander,
*Hemidactylium
scutatum*

53. Many-lined salamander, *Stereochilus marginatus*

54. Gulf Coast mud salamander, *Pseudotriton montanus flavissimus*

55. Rusty mud salamander, *Pseudotriton montanus floridanus*, adult

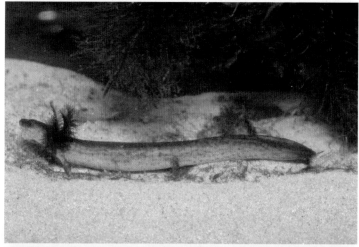

55a. Rusty mud salamander, *Pseudotriton montanus floridana*, larva

56. Southern red salamander, *Pseudotriton ruber vioscai*

57. Southeastern slimy salamander, *Plethodon grobmani*

58. Eastern
Gulf Coast
waterdog,
*Necturus*
species cf
*beyeri*

59. Red-
striped newt,
*Notophthal-
mus perstria-
tus*, adult

59a. Red-
striped newt,
*Notoph-
thalmus
perstriuatus*,
paedomorph

60. Central
newt,
*Notophthalmus
viridescens
louisianensis*

61. Peninsula
newt,
*Notophthalmus
viridescens
piaropicola*

62. Narrow-
striped dwarf
siren, *Pseudo-
branchus axan-
thus axanthus*

63. Everglades
dwarf siren,
*Pseudobran-
chus axanthus
bellii*

64. Broad-
striped dwarf
siren, *Pseu-
dobranchus
striatus striatus*

65. Gulf
Hammock
dwarf siren,
*Pseudobran-
chus striatus
lustricolus*

66. Slender
dwarf siren,
*Pseudobran-
chus striatus
spheniscus*

67. Eastern lesser siren, *Siren intermedia intermedia*

67a. Western lesser siren, *Siren intermedia nettingi*

68. Greater siren, *Siren lacertina*

69. Pickerel frog, *Rana palustris*

70. Spotted salamander, *Ambystoma maculatum*

71. Three-toed amphiuma, *Amphiuma tridactylum*

# Salamanders

## Order Caudata

Despite being often thought otherwise, Florida—at least northern Florida—has a substantial salamander population. A total of 6 families containing 27 described species occur in suitable habitats. When subspecies are considered, Florida's salamander fauna jumps to 32 in number. Two additional species, the three-toed amphiuma and the spotted salamander, and one subspecies, the western lesser siren, occur so close to the Florida state line in Alabama or Georgia that additional field work might find one or both in the Sunshine State. The first two species are described in chapter 3, Peripheral Amphibian Species, and a comment regarding

the western lesser siren is included in species account 67, eastern lesser siren.

All salamanders found in Florida are native species, with no established introduced taxa at this time.

Florida salamanders are of diverse appearance, but all, despite other morphological differences, lack scales and claws. Beyond that generality, identification is best accomplished by looking at family characteristics in the key (page 10) and then at the species descriptions.

Some of Florida's salamanders can be difficult to identify. One key indicator of a salamander's family is the presence (or lack) of a nasolabial groove—a groove extending from the nostril to the lip (and may end in downward-projecting nasal cirri). The nasolabial groove is present only in the lungless salamanders (family Plethodontidae), the salamanders that absorb oxygen through their thin, moist mucous membranes and skin.

## Tigers on a Christmas Eve

In 2004, we sat in our car, listening to the rain patter down as we waited for a lull in traffic so we could pull out. It was about 10 p.m. on Christmas Eve, and I could not help but wonder where all these cars were going tonight. I did not want them here. "Don't they have someplace to BE at this hour?" I asked Dick resentfully. We had somewhere to go, and we were already there—looking for tiger salamanders to cross the tarmac and head toward their breeding pond, just to the north of us. With heavy traffic, the chances of the creatures making it safely across the pavement were dim indeed. What driver is looking out for 8-inch black-and-yellow salamanders on the roadway while headed from point A to point B at 45 miles an hour—on a Christmas Eve—and maybe even after a Christmas party?

Part of the difficulty was that the family of mole salamanders as a group are creatures of habit. As the sea turtles do, the adults return to their natal ponds—the ponds where they hatched—to breed and lay eggs. It's as if they are programmed at birth to return to their birth site, which is of course, the birth site of their parents, and of their parents' parents, and their parents' parents' parents. . . . You can joke and say, "if it's good enough for my dad, it's

*continued*

good enough for me," but things (especially habitats) have a way of quickly changing in Florida.

The male tiger salamanders arrive a few days ahead of the females (no one knows how they figure the timing). The males enter the pond, attach a few spermataphores (sperm packets atop a slender stalk, looking a bit like tiny marshmallows on sticks) to the pond bottom, and wait nearby. When the females arrive, again usually during a cold rain, the males act like guys at a singles bar when a busload of females arrive. They urge the females, with nudges of their chin, over to the tiny area with their sperm packets. "Hey, baby, you're a pretty one, c'mon over here and take a look at these . . ." The females each pick up a spermatophore and deposit their now-fertilized eggs. Males and females then depart and wander the sandy hillsides, slurping up earthworms and insects until next year, when they are again summoned by unseen forces back to their natal ponds.

Once upon a time, tiger salamanders flourished in a certain area in Alachua County—very near where Dick and I now sat in our car. They occupied one particular seasonal pond, returning to breed and lay eggs, then departing to burrow through the sandy flatlands south of the ponds for the rest of the year.

As time went on, human populations grew and the dirt road was paved, then widened and paved again. Adult tiger salamanders who headed northward, across the pavement to their natal pond, might be lucky enough to reach the pond, reproduce, and return to their home range. They might be lucky a few years in a row. But as time went on, crushed bodies on the roadway made it evident that fewer and fewer tigers made it to the pond, and fewer made it back to their home range.

As Dick and I drove the roadway that night, hoping to photograph and move tigers making the breeding trek across the roadway, we found and were able to hasten only two. The next year, Dick was by himself and found only three, all DOR (dead on road). The next year he found none, and the year after that, again none. We placed traps in the pond in the hopes of finding a few in residence, but none turned up. Light rainfall the past few years has meant the pond has stayed dry.

We wonder frequently about the fate of this tiger salamander population.

In Florida a few salamander species are slender and eel-like, but most species are rather lizardlike in proportions. Some are permanently aquatic, but many pass through first an aquatic then a terrestrial stage. Most, but not all, terrestrial salamanders of Florida return to the water to breed and for egg deposition.

Florida's salamanders vary in size, from the tiny, slender dwarf salamander (typically adult at 2½–3 inches) to the comparatively gigantic two-toed amphiuma, which may exceed 3½ feet in length.

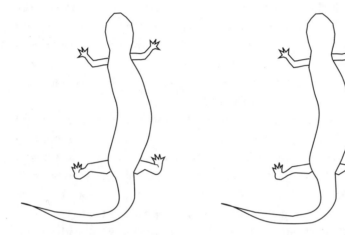

Chunky hind legs of dusky salamander      Slender hind legs of woodland salamander

## MOLE SALAMANDERS: FAMILY AMBYSTOMATIDAE

There are five species of this family in Florida. A sixth, the spotted salamander (see account 70), may eventually be found here. The five species are two taxa of flatwoods salamanders plus the marbled, the mole, and the tiger salamanders. While the first four are rather small, the foot-long tiger salamander bears the distinction of being the largest terrestrial salamander not only in Florida, but in the eastern United States as well.

The designation "mole" as the family name comes from the propensity of all members of this family to burrow. The mole salamanders in Florida are cold-weather breeders. They are induced to gather near breeding ponds by heavy rains of late autumn or winter, usually not until after a few weeks of cold weather. The female marbled salamander selects soon-to-be-flooded situations for egg placement. Whether instinct or site-fidelity leads her to the deposition site is speculative. The two species of flatwoods salamanders place their eggs at water's edge, in the shallows, or in crayfish burrows that retain at least a little water but flood when winter rains begin. The breeding strategies of these three taxa, therefore, differ from those of the other two Florida ambystomatids as well as the peripheral spotted salamander.

Once the ambystomatids leave the breeding ponds, their lives are cloaked in mystery. All species are badly in need of study.

Ambystomatid salamanders are difficult to sex. During the breeding season, reproductively active males develop a conspicuously swollen vent. Only at that time is the external appearance of the adults sufficiently different for gender determination. Immatures and nonbreeding adults cannot be sexed externally.

Both flatwoods salamanders and the tiger salamander are considered uncommon in Florida and seem to be diminishing in numbers. The mole and the marbled salamanders remain relatively common.

# 37. Reticulated Flatwoods Salamander

*Ambystoma bishopi*

**Size:** This newly described species attains a length of 3–3¾ inches.

**Identification:** This is a dark brown to black salamander with a variable but often strongly reticulate white pattern. Morphological differences from the frosted flatwoods salamander (account 38) are present but difficult to ascertain. For the most part, *Ambystoma bishopi* is slightly smaller, has proportionately shorter legs, has a proportionately smaller head, and may have fewer costal grooves.

**Habitat/Range:** Ephemeral pine flatwoods and savanna ponds free of predatory fish are the breeding sites of this salamander. Burrowing crayfish are also usually found at these sites. The salamanders utilize the crayfish burrows and similar subsurface moisture-retaining habitats.

This salamander ranges through the Florida panhandle from west of the Apalachicola River to eastern Mobile Bay. It occurs also in southwestern Georgia.

**Abundance:** This imperiled salamander is federally threatened.

**Behavior:** This is a typical autumn-breeding mole salamander in every sense of the word. During damp weather, adults are occasionally found beneath fallen trunks and other woodland debris; however, at most times they are burrowed more deeply below the ground. Damp crayfish tunnels serve as refuges for breeding and nonbreeding adults.

**Reproduction:** Egg deposition occurs during passage of late autumn or early winter storm systems. The courtship activities occur at night on land or in grassy shallows and consist mostly of the males herding the females toward the sperm packets they've previously deposited in damp areas. The courtship induces the female to straddle a sperm packet and pick it up with her cloacal labia. The female then selects damp to wet shoreline areas, grassy shallows, or a crayfish burrow to distribute her 75–150 eggs singly or in small clusters. The eggs hatch two to three days after being immersed.

**Similar Species:** The frosted flatwoods salamander is very similar but occurs east of the Apalachicola/Chattahoochee River and tends to have a less precise pattern. The marbled salamander has broad light crossbars that often broaden and touch on the sides.

**Comments:** The elevation of the reticulated flatwoods salamander to species level was based on genetic assessment. Use range as the primary identifying factor to distinguish it from the frosted flatwoods salamander.

# 38. Frosted Flatwoods Salamander

*Ambystoma cingulatum*

**Size:** The frosted flatwoods salamander is one of the smaller of the ambystomatids. It is adult at about 3 inches in total length but occasionally attains 4 inches.

**Identification:** The dorsal ground color is dark, varying from black-ish brown to black. The pattern is usually a busy silvery white to white frosted pattern. The lower sides and venter are dark but peppered with white(ish) flecks or spots. The slender, attenuate dark larvae, rather non-descript at first, develop prominent light vertebral and lateral lines. The cheek is light. At this stage they are very pretty and easily identifiable but become less diagnosable as the pattern fragments at metamorphosis.

**Habitat:** This species burrows in the soils of seasonally flooded natural pine and wiregrass flatwoods and breeds in associated shallow ponds and cypress heads. Frosted flatwoods salamanders are known to utilize crayfish burrows as retreats and egg deposition sites. This species occurs east of the Apalachicola/Chattahoochee River from northern Florida to southeastern South Carolina.

**Abundance:** The rare, federally threatened frosted flatwoods salamander once occurred from Marion County northward to Duval and Baker counties. It is now absent from many of its historic sites.

**Behavior:** This is a typical autumn-breeding mole salamander. During damp weather, adults can occasionally be found beneath fallen trunks and other woodland debris; however, at most times they are burrowed more deeply below the ground. Damp crayfish tunnels serve as refuges for the adults.

**Reproduction:** Egg-laying by this species occurs during the passage of late autumn or early winter storm systems. The nudging and bumping courtship activities occur at night on land or in grassy shallows. The courtship induces the female to pick up a previously deposited sperm packet with her cloacal labia. The female then usually selects damp to wet shoreline areas, grassy shallows, or the burrows of crayfish to lay her 75–150 eggs. The eggs are deposited singly or in small clusters. When immersed the eggs hatch in two to three days.

**Similar Species:** Adult marbled salamanders have a proportionately larger head and better-defined, broader dorsal crossbars. Larval marbled salamanders have dorsolateral spots and less prominent stripes than flat-woods salamander larvae. The reticulated flatwoods salamander is very similar but occurs west of the Apalachicola/Chattahoochee River.

**Comments:** As agricultural entities and inhibited burning allow veg-etational succession to alter more and more natural pine and wiregrass flatwoods, the flatwoods salamander is becoming increasingly uncom-mon. It cannot exist in drained areas or deepened ponds. Larvae of the

flatwoods salamander may still be found in some numbers in a few isolated ponds and cypress heads, but extensive searches have shown other
historic sites to be devoid of these beautiful salamanders. The adults are
always more difficult to find than the larvae.

# 39. Marbled Salamander

*Ambystoma opacum*

**Size:** Marbled salamanders are adult at 3–4 inches in total length.

**Identification:** When adult, this beautiful little salamander is sexually
dimorphic. While the dorsal ground color of both sexes is black, the
bands of the female are gray or silver, and those of the male white. Sides
and venter are unrelieved black. Marbled salamanders are short tailed,
stocky, and broad headed.

The larvae are buff to green and have a somewhat darker dorsal stripe,
usually with some evidence of banding or spotting.

**Habitat/Range:** Marbled salamanders occur in Florida in damp hardwood hammocks, usually in river floodplains. We have frequently found
them beneath moisture-retaining trash as well as under and in molder-
ing logs. They require ephemeral ponds for breeding. Although this species now seems confined to the panhandle and the Suwannee River valley, it was once found at least 125 miles south of there. In the mid-1960s,
one of the authors (RDB) found two examples beneath debris under an
isolated railroad bridge near Lithia Springs (Hillsborough County).

**Abundance:** This was once the most widely distributed of Florida's mole
salamanders and may still be the most commonly seen. The reason might
be that the marbled salamander is less persistently fossorial than other
mole salamanders, or at least it doesn't dig as deeply as some.

**Behavior:** Although it is a burrower in damp woodlands, the marbled
salamander often surfaces during rains. It may be encountered crossing
roads after dark, during or after storms.

**Reproduction:** This pretty salamander is an autumn breeder. Courtship, which consists of nudging, butting, and chin-rubs, occurs in damp

terrestrial situations. Males deposit spermatophores at the bases of grass clumps or beneath leaves. These are picked up by females with their cloacal labia. A female then seeks a damp, protected place in a soon-to-be-flooded woodland depression and deposits her clutch of 30 to more than 100 clustered but single eggs in a scooped-out depression in the ground (often of her construction). Until autumn rains flood the depression and immerse the eggs, the female remains in attendance of the clutch. The eggs hatch one to several days following immersion, and from that point on, development is normal. Larvae overwinter in the ponds.

**Similar Species:** The flatwoods salamanders have narrow, less precise markings, a narrow head, and a proportionately longer tail.

**Comments:** This small and pretty salamander is the most strongly dimorphic of any of Florida's ambystomatid species. Although fully capable of burrowing, marbled salamanders often remain rather close to the surface of the ground except during extended droughts.

# 40. Mole Salamander

*Ambystoma talpoideum*

**Size:** This is another of the smaller ambystomatids. Mole salamanders are adult at 3–4½ inches in total length.

**Identification:** The adult mole salamander has a short body, a short tail, and, when adult, a proportionately immense head and feet. This salamander may be dark brown, dark gray, or nearly black with bluish or silvery flecks dorsally and laterally. The light-flecked belly and lower sides are lighter than the dorsum.

The rather nondescript larva is buff to gray, blotched or mottled with darker pigment dorsally or laterally, but has a distinctive unpigmented midventral stripe.

**Habitat:** This persistent burrower is a denizen of damp pine, mixed, or hardwood woodlands. It breeds in temporary woodland ponds.

**Abundance:** This remains a rather common but locally distributed ambystomatid. The range of the mole salamander in Florida includes the northern one-third of the peninsula (from Marion County northward) and the entire panhandle. Populations are increasingly rare at the southern extreme of the range.

**Behavior:** Both the common and specific names call attention to the burrowing habits of this small but robust salamander. Despite its propensity for burrowing, mole salamanders are seen on the surface of the ground (especially during and following hard rains) with some degree of regularity.

**Reproduction:** In Florida the mole salamander accesses its breeding ponds during the heavy rains that accompany winter cold fronts. Males attach stalked spermatophores to leaves, twigs, rocks, or similar litter on pond bottoms. Following a nudging, bumping, chin-rubbing courtship, the female picks the sperm packet from the spermatophore with her cloacal labia. She then deposits eggs in several small clusters until the total clutch of 100 or more is laid. The egg clusters are attached to stems or twigs.

**Similar Species:** No other mole salamander in the United States has the hypertrophied head of the adult mole salamander.

# 41. Eastern Tiger Salamander

*Ambystoma tigrinum*

**Size:** At up to 12 inches in total length, the eastern tiger salamander is the largest terrestrial salamander of the east. Florida specimens seem to be a bit smaller, attaining a length of 7–9 inches. Larvae often attain a length of 6 or more inches prior to metamorphosing.

**Identification:** Eastern tiger salamanders are of variable color and pattern. Many Florida examples are sparsely spotted, and in many cases the spots do not contrast sharply with the ground color. The dorsal ground color varies from brown to nearly black. The light dorsal and lateral spots are of irregular shape and arrangement and seem never to be in the rather precise rows seen on the smaller spotted salamander. The light spots can vary from an off-white or cream to a rather intense butter yellow or olive green. The belly is light (light olive to yellow) with dark markings.

Larvae are often an unrelieved olive brown dorsally and laterally and somewhat lighter ventrally.

**Habitat/Range:** Although they are known to occur in diverse woodland habitats, tiger salamanders are so faithful to a breeding site that draining or deepening a single ancestral breeding pond may destroy an entire population. Moderately to heavily vegetated ponds are preferred. These must contain no predatory fish. Adult tiger salamanders burrow deeply into yielding loamy soils but may be most common in sandy pinelands. This species occurs locally in suitable habitat in the northwestern one-third of peninsular Florida as well as throughout the panhandle.

**Abundance:** In Florida this is a rarely seen salamander. Wetland destruction and heavily trafficked roadways near ancestral breeding sites make no allowances for this creature. It has seemingly been extirpated in several areas where it once occurred.

**Behavior:** Adult tiger salamanders are extensively fossorial and rarely seen. On the infrequent occasions when they do emerge from their burrows, they do so at night. Occasionally they wander into swimming pools or other such "traps" from which it is difficult to escape. The larvae are occasionally netted in ponds.

**Reproduction:** In north Florida, tiger salamanders are activated and induced into breeding migrations by heavy winter rains. Usually these occur during the passage of a frontal system that markedly lowers barometric pressure and that has been preceded by a week or two of rather cold weather. As with many ambystomatids, male tiger salamanders usually enter the breeding ponds before the females and may remain in the ponds for many days longer than the females, which again depart the water for the woodlands soon after laying. The eggs are large, and the clump may contain as few as 25 to more than 100 eggs. The larvae often attain a length of 4–6 inches before metamorphosing.

**Similar Species:** The spotted salamander, not yet known from Florida, has rounded, more regularly arranged spots.

**Comments:** Because populations seem to be declining, the tiger salamanders of Florida are in need of nearly continuous monitoring. Because of their fidelity to a breeding site, it is particularly important that breeding ponds and accesses to the ponds are preserved.

## AMPHIUMAS: FAMILY AMPHIUMIDAE

Although they are common, the aquatic amphiumas are so persistently nocturnal and secretive that their presence in any body of water is easily overlooked.

Of the three described species, two are well known in Florida, and the third nears our borders.

These are slender, attenuate salamanders that have four tiny legs. Their common names combine the number of toes on each foot (not, by the way, an infallible method of ascertaining a positive identification) with the generic name *Amphiuma,* but in common parlance, amphiuma is not capitalized. Both the one-toed and two-toed amphiumas occur in Florida, and the three-toed amphiuma nears the Florida state line in south central Alabama. Early records of the three-toed amphiuma found on the western panhandle are probably in error.

While little is known with certainty about the natural history of the one-toed amphiuma, the lives of the two and three-toed amphiumas are a bit more thoroughly researched.

# 42. Two-toed Amphiuma

*Amphiuma means*

**Size:** Most two-toed amphiumas seen are in the 8–20-inch range. Exceptional adults may exceed 3½ feet in total length.

**Identification:** Two-toed amphiuma are dark mud gray dorsally, lighter ventrally, and have no well-defined line of demarcation between the two colors. Hatchlings are black (or nearly so) dorsally.

As the common name implies, the tiny legs are *usually* tipped with two toes each. Occasional examples with one and/or three toes have been found.

The nose is rounded when viewed from above but flattened in profile. The eyes are small, nonprotuberant, and lidless. Prior to shedding, the

## Where, Oh Where, Do the One-toes Go?

When any of my friends suggests we go mudding, the term has a different meaning than it does for most folks. We don't clamber into mud-splattered high-wheeled trucks and head for the nearest sanctioned mud bog; rather, we gather up dredge (not that we're often able to use it), potato rake, and bucket and head to some little mud seepage in hopes of finding one or two specific species of salamanders. In short, mudding to us connotes a search, often in soupy mud up to our knees while hoping we don't unexpectedly step into a deeper pocket, for the very locally distributed one-toed amphiuma.

The one-toed amphiuma is the smallest and most poorly understood of the three species in this genus. Compared with the habitat preferred by the one-toed amphiuma, the habitat of the other two species is aquatic, and they can be found in swamps, marshes, rivers, streams, ditches, seeps, flooded prairies, ponds, lakes, and whatever other bodies of water I've left out.

One-toed amphiumas, however, occur in seepages with muddy edges and bottoms with the consistency of a slurry of mud soup, and these little eel-like salamanders don't seem to tolerate much variation in the slurry. We know of a couple of areas that have proven pretty good locales for the amphiuma, where we might, within minutes, find one, two, or even three. But if time allows and we try our luck again a week or two later, even though the slurry may look the same to us, it might produce no salamanders. We have learned that if for some reason an inch or two of water lies atop the slurry to simply turn around and walk away. We will find no one-toed amphiuma in those conditions.

Where do these little salamanders hie to when not in the slurry? We have no idea. Perhaps they follow root systems back into better-drained areas. Perhaps they have burrows of their own to which they retreat. And perhaps we will never know. It is this wondering and a hope of learning that keeps us returning to amphiuma-ville time and again.

salamander assumes a bluish color and the eyes become opaque. An oval or elliptical gill opening is present on each side of the head.

**Habitat/Range:** The shallows of lakes, ponds, streams, ditches, rivers—even some deeper areas of straight-sided drainage canals—may all harbor sizable populations of two-toed amphiumas. These salamanders seem most at home in silted or heavily vegetated waters, amidst detritus, or in areas with easily burrowed muddy bottoms.

**Abundance:** When coupled with their secretive behavior and aquatic lifestyle, the nocturnal activity patterns of the two-toed amphiuma easily explain why these salamanders are not more often seen or readily recognized by Floridians. While populations may not be dense, two-toed amphiumas dwell in most aquatic habitats throughout the state. They do not occur in the Keys.

**Behavior:** Two-toed amphiumas will bite, and bite strongly, both in a feeding response or when carelessly restrained. The strong jaws, powerful enough to crush crayfish, frogs, and small snakes, require respect. If a relatively stationary object such as a finger is grasped, the salamander will rotate on its long axis, peeling the skin away. Stitches may be necessary to repair the damage done to a human appendage. Amphiuma may occur in ponds that occasionally dry. When ponds dry, in a manner similar to that of sirens and lungfishes, the salamanders burrow deeply into the bottom mud, forming cocoons that retain moisture almost perfectly to await the return of the rains. These interesting salamanders may be found foraging by night in shallows or in thick mats of vegetation. Besides the already mentioned items, amphiuma eat all manner of aquatic insects, worms, fish and their eggs, and other aquatic organisms.

**Reproduction:** The water-edge or shallow-water nesting site is usually beneath a log, a board, or matted vegetation or is similarly concealed. If water level recedes, the nests may be left some distance from the water. The beadlike string of 150 or so jelly-covered eggs is often folded into a flattened ball. The female amphiuma remains with the eggs during the several-month incubation. For a short time after hatching, hatchling amphiuma have barely discernible external gills. Hatchlings are about 1½ inches in total length. Females in south Florida lay their eggs during the winter or early spring months. Those in north Florida lay in late spring or early summer.

**Similar Species:** To date, the three-toed amphiuma is not known in Florida. The one-toed amphiuma is much smaller, has a more rounded head profile, only one toe on each of the four very tiny feet, and is adapted to a habitat of oozy black mud rather than open water. Sirens of all species have external gills throughout their lives and lack rear legs. American eels (true fish), now rare, have fins and typical gills and gill covers.

**Comments:** Amphiuma are occasionally caught by fishermen. As much because they are believed poisonous as for their writhing and biting, hooked specimens are either cut free with hook and line intact or killed. Large captives will eat prey as diverse as chunks of bologna, crayfish, and adult mice.

# 43. One-toed Amphiuma

*Amphiuma pholeter*

**Size:** This is the smallest of the three species in this genus. *Amphiuma pholeter* appears to be adult at between 9 and 10 inches in length and tops out at just about 12 inches.

**Identification:** This salamander is nearly uniformly dark brown or blackish brown both dorsally and laterally and only slightly (if at all) lighter ventrally. The legs of *A. pholeter* are proportionately the tiniest of those of any member of the genus, and each foot is tipped with one toe. Two oval gill openings, one on each side, are located posterior of the head. The snout is weakly convex in profile. The eyes are lidless and nonprotuberant.

**Habitat/Range:** The one-toed amphiuma dwells in deep beds of soupy, organic muck—a particularly difficult habitat to sample. Because of this anaerobic habitat, it has been nearly impossible to learn any details of the life history of this salamander. It occurs in suitable habitats across the panhandle, southward to the Gulf Hammock area on Florida's northwestern peninsula.

**Abundance:** The true population statistics of this salamander remain unknown, but if searched for specifically, it is not particularly hard to find.

**Behavior:** This streamside, muckland salamander is seldom seen unless raked or otherwise dislodged from its mud-bed microhabitat. Many invertebrates also occur in such habitat, and it is probable that small worms, mollusks, and insects are the food of the one-toed amphiuma. It is unknown where these salamanders go when water levels rise and cover their habitats, but habitats that usually harbor a fair number will yield few or none when water levels are high. Certainly decreased visibility during times of high water figures prominently in the inability of researchers to find specimens. Researchers have referred to the habitat of this salamander in high-water periods as "liquid slurry" and at other times as having the consistency of chocolate pudding.

**Reproduction:** Much about the breeding biology of this species remains conjectural. It is thought that *A. pholeter* lays its eggs in the early summer and that, like the other members of the genus, the female attends the eggs until hatching. Clutch size is unknown.

**Similar Species:** Sirens have external gills and no hind legs. The two-toed amphiuma is larger and has a lighter belly, and a flattened snout, and usually two toes on each foot. The three-toed amphiuma has not yet been found in Florida.

# LUNGLESS SALAMANDERS: FAMILY PLETHODONTIDAE

This family contains a hodgepodge of salamanders and is represented in Florida by 13 diverse species. These fall into two groups (subfamilies), the dusky salamanders, subfamily Desmognathinae, with four Florida species, and the Plethodontinae, comprising the remaining 9 species.

Attempting identification of the dusky salamanders will prove at very least an exercise in true dedication and at worst an exercise in futility. It is most often necessary to note negative rather than positive characteristics. Duskies are easily separated from the other plethodontids, but less easily from each other. Knowing the geographic origin of a specimen is the first step. Tail shape, taken in cross section, is an important consideration. All members of the dusky salamander group have hind legs that are much stouter than the forelegs, a characteristic not shared with members of the subfamily Plethodontinae. Dusky salamanders have a light line running diagonally rearward from the eye to the angle of the jaws. Additionally, although it is less often observable, the jaw structure differs between the two groups. Dusky salamanders open their mouths by lifting the top of the head rather than by dropping the lower jaw, rather disconcerting the first time you see it.

In all plethodontids the lungs are lacking. Respiration is accomplished through the skin and mucous membranes, which must always be moist. The salamanders in this family have a nasolabial groove. In males of some species the grooves extend onto downward projections called nasal cirri. The cirri are visible during the breeding season on such Florida species as the southern two-lined salamander.

All the plethodontids usually hide by day (some may be active during overcast or rainy weather, especially when barometric pressure is dropping during passage of a frontal system) but emerge to forage on damp or dewy nights. Some species are largely restricted to the environs of springs or creeks; others wander rather far afield but are *always* in damp areas and microhabitats.

Florida plethodontids range in size from the slender 2¾-inch dwarf salamander to the more robust 6-inch southern red salamander.

The reproductive strategies of the salamanders in this group are variable. One constant in both aquatic and terrestrial plethodontids is the "tail-straddling walk." In this, following stimulation, a female closely follows, and straddles with her forelegs, the tail of a walking male about to deposit a spermatophore. The male may stimulate the female by nudging or rubbing her with his chin to transfer secretions from the mental (chin) gland, or by dragging his mental gland and teeth along her nape and shoulder area. At the culmination of the tail-straddling walk, the male deposits the spermatophore; the female walks over it and picks the spermcap off with her cloacal labia. Egg-laying follows.

The most divergent of the Florida plethodontid species in external appearance is the Georgia blind salamander, a troglodytic paedomorph (physiologically unable to metamorphose but as a larva becomes sexually mature and reproduces) that seems far more common in the caverns of Florida than in its namesake state.

Details of the life histories of most plethodontids are sparse. All species are badly in need of extended field studies.

Dusky Salamanders: Subfamily Desmognathinae

## 44. Apalachicola Dusky Salamander

*Desmognathus apalachicolae*

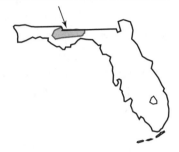

**Size:** Although occasional specimens near 4 inches in total length, most found are between 2½ and 3½ inches long.

**Identification:** The term "nondescript" best describes this and most other dusky salamanders. *Desmognathus apalachicolae* may be unicolored (older examples) or rather prominently spotted or blotched (younger examples). If patterned, the spots are often outlined on their outer edges with some black pigment. The spots may be discrete or coalesce into bands or even stripes. The dorsal ground color is brown(ish). The venter is usually white but may show traces of dark pigment. Except at its tip where it is attenuate and compressed, the long tail is nearly round in cross section.

Larvae netted from leaves submerged in the shallows of a stream were brownish dorsally and had vague dorsal spotting and a very low tail fin.

**Habitat:** Deep and relatively cool ravines having extensive carpets of sphagnum moss and permanent clear streams are home to the Apalachicola dusky salamander.

**Abundance:** In its very limited range, this is not an uncommon salamander. In Florida the Apalachicola dusky salamander will be encountered only near the Georgia state line in the drainages of the Ochlockonee and Apalachicola rivers.

**Behavior:** Secretive by day, the Apalachicola dusky salamander may forage on the top of sphagnum mats and even climb up 12 inches or more into low herbaceous plants at night.

**Reproduction:** Egg clutches with a female in attendance, containing about 10 ova each, were found beneath a sphagnum-covered limb at the edge of a stream in a deep ravine in Liberty County.

**Similar Species:** Two confusingly similar species are found within the range of the Apalachicola dusky salamander, the southern dusky salamander and the spotted dusky salamander. In cross section the tails of both are teardrop shaped. The southern dusky salamander has a dark venter, while the belly of the spotted dusky salamander is light but prominently flecked with black.

**Comments:** Range and its deep ravine/sphagnum bog microhabitat are at least as important as appearance in identifying this species.

# 45. Southern Dusky Salamander

*Desmognathus auriculatus*

**Size:** Most southern dusky salamanders seen are in the 3½–5-inch size range. Rarely a specimen attains or barely exceeds 6 inches.

**Identification:** This salamander is dark brown to nearly black dorsally and laterally, with a white spotted dark belly. Although some specimens (particularly older ones) may be largely devoid of lateral markings, most have one or two irregular rows of small whitish, cream, or orangish spots ("portholes") on each side. The tails of some specimens have an orangish or buff upper edge. The tail is teardrop shaped (in cross section) near the body but more strongly compressed with a sharp upper edge posteriorly.

The larvae are very dark dorsally, have a translucent belly skin, and may have indications of the light-colored portholes on their sides.

**Habitat/Range:** The range of the southern dusky salamander once extended from the vicinity of Tampa Bay northward beyond the Georgia state line and throughout the panhandle, then westward. Its current range has not been adequately mapped, but it is recognized that since 1990 many populations have been decimated or extirpated. Look for this salamander beneath creek-edge fallen limbs, rocks, and leaf mats.

**Abundance:** Once common, now rare.

**Behavior:** Southern dusky salamanders prefer a wet microhabitat and hide beneath debris in shallow water or at water's edge. They may forage widely on rainy or foggy evenings, especially during the passage of frontal systems that drop barometric pressure.

**Reproduction:** A southern dusky salamander attends the clutch of one to three dozen eggs throughout the 30-day incubation period. The egg cluster (actually a folded string) is laid in the late summer or autumn beneath wet to saturated leaf mats or in the mud beneath a log or rock.

**Similar Species:** The Apalachicola dusky salamander has a tail round in cross section basally. The spotted dusky salamander lacks small, light round spots (often termed "portholes") on its sides and tends to bear a more colorful dorsal pattern.

**Comments:** Although southern dusky salamanders are now drastically reduced in numbers, some populations appear to be increasing slightly. Immediate studies are needed to determine the cause of population reductions. The agent(s) affecting the populations of this salamander may also be affecting those of other species.

# 46. Spotted Dusky Salamander

*Desmognathus conanti*

**Size:** Although not large, the spotted dusky salamander is of rather robust build. While most adults are smaller, spotted duskies occasionally attain an overall length of somewhat more than 4½ inches.

**Identification:** While it should be kept in mind that no dusky salamander of Florida is brightly colored, some examples of this species are more brightly colored than others. The sides are tan, and the dorsum may be brown or buff with or without dark-edged irregularly paired brighter buff to dull golden or orangish spots. The belly is white(ish) but variably patterned with light and/or dark pepperings. The tail is teardrop shaped in cross section.

The larvae are dark and not too dissimilar in appearance from the adults they will become.

**Habitat/Range:** Although outside Florida the spotted dusky salamander is found in a wide variety of habitats, in Florida it is most commonly encountered near springs and the edges of clear streams in the ravines of the western panhandle.

**Abundance:** The spotted dusky salamander is a locally common species in suitable habitat. It ranges from Florida's Leon and Wakulla counties westward to and beyond the Alabama line.

**Behavior:** Like most small salamanders, the spotted dusky hides by day and forages by night.

**Reproduction:** The clusters of 8–30 eggs are laid beneath a rock, log, or mat of vegetation at the edge of a stream on very wet ground. The bottom eggs of the clutch may actually be in the water. The females usually remain in attendance of the eggs through the 30–40-day incubation period. The gilled larvae may develop in shallow water but as often as not are found in mats of very wet but not submerged leaves or sphagnum.

**Similar Species:** This can be a difficult salamander to identify. Its tail is less compressed than the southern dusky, but more so than that of the Apalachicola dusky. It is also often more brightly colored than either. See the comments in the species accounts for the Apalachicola dusky salamander (account 44) and the southern dusky salamander (account 45).

**Comments:** As a group, dusky salamanders are difficult to identify. Some examples of the Apalachicola dusky salamander closely approach the spotted dusky in appearance. Tail shape (in cross section), habitat, and range are important tools in field identification of these salamanders.

# 47. Seal Salamander

*Desmognathus monticola*

**Size:** The Florida specimens of this salamander are smaller than those in the Appalachians. Florida specimens seem to top out at about 4½ inches in total length.

**Identification:** The dorsum of young adults is often mottled buff and olive brown. The sides are abruptly lighter. The venter is also light. A row of light flecks or dots extends along each side from front to hind legs. There is a tendency for seal salamanders to become darker and more unicolored both dorsally and ventrally with advancing age.

The larvae and newly transformed juveniles often have four or five pairs of light dorsolateral dots on the trunk and additional light dots on the tail.

**Habitat:** In Florida, seal salamanders are known only from a single very restricted area having streams with rocky bottoms in cool ravines in Escambia County. The aquatic larvae are found in gravelly areas of streams.

**Abundance:** This is an uncommon species in Florida.

**Behavior:** Seal salamanders may be found beneath litter or in burrows by day but often leave their areas of seclusion to forage by night.

**Reproduction:** The two dozen or more eggs of this rather aquatic salamander are attached to the bottoms of flat rocks or more rarely logs in seepages and similar areas. The female remains in attendance of her clutch throughout the lengthy incubation period.

**Similar Species:** The range of the much slenderer Apalachicola dusky salamander is well to the east of that of the seal salamander. The ranges of the southern and spotted dusky salamanders overlap the range of the seal salamander; see accounts 45 and 46.

**Comments:** In Florida, this uncommon salamander may occasionally be seen at night on the edges of the streams it inhabits.

## Brook Salamander Group: Subfamily Plethodontinae

# 48. Southern Two-lined Salamander

*Eurycea cirrigera*

**Size:** Although this species may attain a length of 4 inches, its extreme slenderness makes it look much smaller.

**Identification:** This pretty variable salamander is rather easily recognized. The dorsal color varies from grayish tan or buff to a very bright orange. The brightest examples are often found atop bluffs in sandy habitats during the breeding season. The lateral color may be the same as that of the dorsum on the paler specimens, but somewhat paler than the dorsum on the orange ones. A black dorsolateral stripe is present on each side, extending from eye to tail tip and usually complete (but may be broken). Vestiges of a dark vertebral stripe may be present. There are 5 toes on each hind foot. Males have well-developed nasal cirri.

The aquatic larvae are quite nondescript when young but develop the characteristic stripes as they age.

**Habitat/Range:** *Eurycea cirrigera* is found beneath natural and man-made litter in and along brooks, streams, and seepages and during wet weather may range well out into damp woodlands. The larvae are common in leafbeds in shallow to moderately deep flowing water. It ranges westward from Dixie and Columbia counties throughout the panhandle to the Alabama state line.

**Abundance:** This is a tiny, pretty, and common salamander.

**Behavior:** Two-lined salamanders are inactive and secretive by day but may forage rather widely at night. They may ascend well above the ground into herbaceous vegetation on damp nights.

**Reproduction:** The two to four dozen stalked single eggs are attached to the underside of stable submerged debris such as stones (which are not common in Florida habitats), submerged logs, and roots. The female remains in attendance of her clutch throughout the two months of incubation.

**Similar Species:** The dwarf salamander is of quite similar appearance but has only 4 toes on each hind foot. The three-lined salamander has a well-developed middorsal stripe.

**Comments:** The larvae of the southern two-lined salamander are abundant in submerged leafbeds in panhandle streams.

# 49. Three-lined Salamander

*Eurycea guttolineata*

**Size:** This is a long-tailed, slender salamander. Adults vary from about 4½ to 7 inches.

**Identification:** The yellowish to buff dorsum is divided by a dark mid-dorsal stripe and bordered at each side by a broad, dark lateral stripe. Infiltration by light pigment may appear in the dark lateral stripes and break into broad vertical bars on the sides of the tail. The vertebral stripe (which may be broken or incomplete) may be variably divided by a thread-thin line of light pigment. The venter is light with a profusion of dark spots. The legs are prominently spotted, and there are 5 toes on each hind foot.

Except for the fact that the vertebral stripe may be weak or, rarely, lacking, the gilled, aquatic larvae are very similar to the adults in appearance.

**Habitat:** This pretty salamander can be particularly common near seepages, grottoes, and caves and is the salamander regularly encountered during cave tours in Florida Caverns State Park. It is also found in damp areas of many hardwood woodlands and along stream and river edges. It occurs from Jefferson County in the eastern panhandle westward and northward to (and beyond) the Alabama and Georgia state lines.

**Abundance:** In suitable habitat the three-lined salamander can be quite common.

**Behavior:** In caves and grottoes this salamander is active around the clock. It climbs the cave walls easily and is adept at finding crevices in which to hide. Outside of caves the three-lined salamander hides by day beneath rocks and logs. It emerges to forage by night.

**Reproduction:** Egg-deposition occurs from late autumn through the months of winter. The several dozen eggs are laid and attached singly to the underside of submerged or water-edge shelters such as rocks or logs, or in subsurface tunnels and passageways. The larvae are aquatic. The female provides nest protection for the month and a half or two months of incubation.

**Similar Species:** The two-lined and dwarf salamanders lack a well-developed vertebral stripe. Dwarf salamanders have only 4 toes on each hind foot.

**Comments:** This is one of the prettiest of Florida's salamanders. It has only recently been afforded full species status. Older texts refer to this salamander as *Eurycea longicauda guttolineata*.

# 50. Dwarf Salamander

*Eurycea quadridigitata*

**Size:** This is a very long-tailed salamander that is adult at less than 3½ inches total length.

**Identification:** This attenuate salamander has a brown dorsum (often with an apparent herringbone pattern) and lighter sides that are separated from each other by a broad, dark dorsolateral stripe. There may be some indication of a darker middorsal stripe. Reproductively active males develop nasal cirri. There are only 4 toes on each hind foot. The gilled larvae are darkest dorsally and when nearing metamorphosis develop a dark dorsolateral line on each side.

**Habitat/Range:** Although the dwarf salamander may wander away from permanent water in the damper woodlands of north Florida, in the seasonally dry south it seems more restricted to the immediate environs of water. This is a common species in the sphagnum beds of north Florida and remains so in the tangles of frogsbit and hydrocotyl roots in the central part of the state. In the south it is associated with dense patches of water lettuce and water hyacinth. It may shelter beneath matted shoreline vegetation or damp logs. On rainy nights adults are often seen crossing roadways parallel to canals, drainage ditches, or vegetation-choked rivers. This small attenuate salamander occurs further southward on Florida's peninsula than any other plethodontid. It has been found from Dade County to well north of the Georgia state line as well as throughout and west of the panhandle.

**Abundance:** Common but only seasonally active above ground in north Florida and on the panhandle, the dwarf salamander seems to be less easily found in the south.

**Behavior:** Over much of Florida these slender salamanders may be seen foraging at night amid floating hyacinths and water lettuce. They may also be encountered at night, at times in numbers, crossing rain-swept roadways. When and where terrestrial, dwarf salamanders may be extensively subterranean, utilizing the burrows of other small creatures during dry weather.

**Reproduction:** Egg deposition occurs from late autumn through the winter months. The one dozen to nearly four dozen eggs are laid singly, but often close to each other in aquatic or water-edge vegetation. Eggs have been found just beneath the waterline on the bladders of hyacinths and on the undersides of the lowest leaves of water lettuce.

**Similar Species:** Except for the uncommon four-toed salamander (known in Florida only from portions of the panhandle), which has an enamel-white belly prominently spotted with black, the dwarf salamander is the only currently described, nongilled (terrestrial) Florida salamander with 4 toes on the hind feet.

**Comments:** Considerable biochemical differences have been found in some populations of these salamanders. It is probable that, as currently understood, this is actually a species complex.

# 51. Georgia Blind Salamander

*Haideotriton wallacei*

**Size:** Most specimens seen are juveniles 1–2 inches long. Occasional 3-inch adults have been seen.

**Identification:** Juveniles of this species are an overall translucent (sometimes pinkish) white with a vague overwash of dark pigment. Adults are pure white. The gills of Georgia blind salamanders of all ages are pink or red. Immature specimens have dark eyespots. These become obscure with advancing age.

**Habitat/Range:** This salamander occurs in ground water (not runoff!) pools in the darkness of caves, and in deep wells and underground solution chambers. It is found in both deep and shallow cave pools in Jackson County, Florida.

**Abundance:** Unknown but probably common where water conditions are pristine. Because of restricted access to its Stygian habitat, population

# A Salamander of Darkness

The stars at night are big and bright—and so the ditty goes.

The words are true when you're in the outside world, which I definitely was not.

I was in a cave, quite deeply in a cave, and I had no idea whether the stars were still bright or not. I remembered that clouds had begun to blot the moon while we were walking to the cave. Maybe by now it was pouring. I sure hoped this was not a cave that was affected adversely by an occasional storm.

A cave is never my favorite place, but if I wished to see a Georgia cave salamander, I had very little say in the matter. The cave, Girard's Cave by name, was huge, but at least it was for the most part dry. Here and there along the edges of the tunnel were little ledged drop-offs that held crystal-clear water, and the bottom was who knew how far down in the blackness below. Translucent amphipods swam to and fro, their presence more apparent from the shadows they cast in the beams of our lights than from the actual sighting of the organism.

As we neared each pool, we slowed and tread very quietly. Ghostly white eyeless crayfish of all sizes, tiny to adult, were abundant in the pools. Since they pretty much ignored the flashlight beams, we hoped the salamander would do so too. Pool followed pool, crayfish followed crayfish. I was now a whole lot further in that I had ever wished to be.

Ahead was another pool, and then the floor of the cave angled upward. By the moment I was becoming less sure that I really wanted to be where I then was. Well, I'd go to the pool anyway. Ed and Lana Vetter, my guides, were already ahead assessing the possibility of making it up the incline. Little did they know I had already decided that was not an option I was going to attempt.

Pool. Amphipods. Crayfish. Some almost at my feet. But it was something on the far side of the pool, on the wall of the cave, that caught my eye. I couldn't even make out what it was, but there was something there. As I watched, a bit of white emerged from the sediment, then a tiny head appeared and then a spindly leg. The something I had first seen transformed as I watched to a salamander about an inch and a half long with big red gills and no eyes.

Ed, Lana, I yelled excitedly. C'mere! Success . . .

statistics for this species can only be guessed. Few adults have been seen, but juvenile specimens are relatively common.

**Behavior:** The blind salamander is a permanently gilled aquatic species. It is very sensitive to disturbances in the water, quickly darting away. Pigmentless troglobitic crayfish and amphipods occur in the same pools as this salamander.

**Reproduction:** Details of reproductive biology are basically unknown, but gravid females have been found in both spring and early winter.

**Similar Species:** None. This is the only blind salamander in Florida.

**Comments:** The first known Georgia blind salamander came from a deep well in Albany, Georgia. Since its discovery, however, far more specimens of this troglobitic paedomorph have been seen in Florida caves than in its namesake state.

## Four-toed and Many-lined Salamanders

# 52. Four-toed Salamander

*Hemidactylium scutatum*

**Size:** This small salamander is adult at 2¼–3 inches in total length. Occasional specimens near 4 inches long.

**Identification:** The four-toed salamander is clad in earthen tones dorsally with a fine but variable peppering of black spots. The belly is enamel white with discrete black spots. There is a basal tail constriction. The top of the tail is often brighter in color than the dorsum. The short nose is bluntly rounded. Larvae are short tailed and of a rather nondescript brown dorsally. The ventral spotting can be seen on nearly mature and mature larvae. The tail fin of the larva extends far forward onto its back.

**Habitat/Range:** Extensive, acidic, sphagnaceous areas and nearby woodlands are the favored habitat of the four-toed salamander. In such habitats four-toed salamanders seek refuge beneath logs, limbs, and debris but seem invariably most common beneath stream-edge sphagnum mats. It is currently known only from the Florida panhandle counties of Gadsden, Leon, Okaloosa, and Walton.

**Abundance:** Very locally distributed but common where found.

**Behavior:** The four-toed salamander is dependent on acidic sphagnaceous areas for survival. It may be turned up beneath sphagnum mats in all but the hottest and driest weather. In many areas north of Florida, the four-toed salamander is known to make autumn breeding migrations; whether it does so in Florida is unknown.

**Reproduction:** Up to three dozen (often fewer) eggs are laid above the water level in sphagnum mats or similar suitable areas. Communal nestings are not uncommon. Females attend the clutch(es) throughout the 1½–2-month incubation period. The short-tailed larvae are aquatic.

**Similar Species:** The only other terrestrial Florida salamander with 4 toes on the hind feet is the dwarf salamander. The dwarf salamander lacks the prominently black-spotted white belly and the basal tail constriction.

**Comments:** This species is badly in need of life history studies in Florida.

# 53. Many-lined Salamander

*Stereochilus marginatus*

**Size:** The many-lined salamander is small, slender, and attenuate. It is adult at about 2½ inches but may occasionally attain a 4-inch overall length.

**Identification:** Despite the reference to many lines in the salamander's common name, the pattern is usually obscure and difficult to perceive. The most discernible markings are a dark stripe from the eye to the back of the head, a dark vertebral line, and dark (often broken) lines on the lower sides. The dorsal ground color of this small salamander is olive brown to yellowish brown. The sides and belly are lighter. The belly has dark flecks. The tail may be a lighter gold brown dorsally. The head is very slender. The larvae are colored similarly to the adults but have external gills.

**Habitat/Range:** The primary habitat of this poorly known salamander is sphagnum and leaf mats growing in acidic backwaters and swamps. Here, it may be found in standing water in and beneath the mats. It may also inhabit swamp- and seepage-edge leaf mats. It occurs only in and near the drainage of Georgia's Okefenokee Swamp in Baker, Columbia, Nassau, and Union counties.

**Abundance:** Following the recent extended droughts in Florida, this small and very secretive salamander, always rare in the state, is now even more so. It appears to have been extirpated by drought from some of its few known locales.

**Behavior:** The many-lined salamander is very secretive, often leaving the water only when it dries. It then seeks seclusion in and beneath rotting logs and in moisture-holding mats of vegetation (including fallen leaves). In general, very little is known about this salamander in Florida.

**Reproduction:** Despite its primarily aquatic lifestyle as both larva and adult, the eggs of the many-lined salamander have been found above the waterline in the decomposing logs that crisscross its swampland habitats. Females lay 10–50 eggs during the winter months. Incubation takes several weeks, during which the female remains in attendance of the eggs.

**Similar Species:** The southern dusky salamander (the only dusky found in the range of the many-lined salamander in Florida) lacks all traces of longitudinal lines and has a dark belly, hind legs stouter than the front legs, a ventrolateral row of light "portholes," and a proportionately broad head.

**Comments:** The many-lined salamander is one of the more primitive of the plethodontids.

Red Salamander Group

## 54. Gulf Coast Mud Salamander

*Pseudotriton montanus flavissimus*

Gulf Coast
Rusty

**Size:** This is the larger and stockier of the two subspecies of mud sala-mander found in Florida. This subspecies nears 5 inches in total length.

**Identification:** Young adults are a rather brilliant black-flecked orange red to salmon dorsally and laterally and have an unmarked pink belly. The tail is yellowish dorsally. The eyes are (usually) relatively dark. The larvae are reddish brown dorsally and variably pinkish ventrally. The venter has dark spots.

All mud salamanders dull in color with advancing age. Some turn a solid brown with an orangish patina.

**Habitat/Range:** The Gulf Coast mud salamander inhabits muddy seeps, spring edges, brook overflows, swamps, and wet lowland hammocks on the western Florida panhandle. All mud salamanders are persistent burrowers.

**Abundance:** Although mud salamanders are secretive, locally distrib-uted, and seldom seen, they are probably not uncommon.

**Behavior:** Mud salamanders are aptly named. They actively burrow through the soupy mud of seepage areas and wet lowland hammocks. As you might surmise, this choice of habitat makes mud salamanders difficult to observe. They also utilize crayfish burrows. Those mud sala-manders that are seen are often deliberately sought by researchers, but adults may sometimes be found crossing roadways on rainy nights.

**Reproduction:** Little is known with certainty about the reproductive biology of either subspecies of the mud salamander in Florida. It is prob-able that the 50–200 eggs are laid beneath partially submerged logs dur-ing the late autumn or early winter months. The female may remain in attendance until hatching. The eggs are thought to take about a month and a half to incubate. The larvae are aquatic. The mud salamanders in some populations breed biennially. It is unknown whether this is the case in Florida.

**Similar Species:** See account #55 for a discussion of the rusty mud salamander. The southern red salamander is stockier and liberally flecked with light spots dorsally and laterally.

55. Rusty Mud Salamander, *Pseudotriton montanus floridanus*, attains a maximum length of 4½ inches; however, most adults are between 3 and 4 inches long. Both the adults and larvae of this southeasternmost race of mud salamander are comparatively dull in coloration. A blotchy patina of dark pigment dulls most of the orange red on the back and sides. The venter is lighter with orange red flecking. This subspecies once ranged from as far south as Orange County to beyond the Georgia-Florida state line, including the eastern panhandle. Some populations seem to have been extirpated.

# 56. Southern Red Salamander

*Pseudotriton ruber vioscai*

**Size:** This is a fairly robust salamander that commonly attains 4½–5½ inches in total length, rarely slightly exceeding 6 inches.

**Identification:** The southern red salamander is the dullest in color of the several races of *Pseudotriton ruber*. This is especially true of old adults. The dorsal and lateral coloration is a pale reddish brown to purplish brown. There is a profusion of light flecks anteriorly and dark speckling posteriorly. The venter is lighter than the dorsum and is black flecked. The iris may be gold or brassy in color, but some are dark. Larvae are similar to the adults in ground color but lack the light and dark flecking.

**Habitat/Range:** In Florida the southern red salamander is associated with acidic, sphagnaceous, hardwood ravines through which flow small streams. The salamanders live in burrows beneath well-settled logs and other woodland litter. During dry periods they seem to be found in the immediate proximity of the streams but disperse somewhat during wet periods. The southern red salamander's main distribution is in the Florida panhandle from Leon County westward, but an apparently disjunct population occurs in Hamilton County.

**Abundance:** Like the mud salamander, the congeneric southern red salamander is locally distributed. Although common in certain habitats, it is seldom seen unless specifically searched for.

**Behavior:** By day this is a secretive salamander, emerging from burrows to forage at night. This is especially true during rainy weather and when barometric pressure is falling.

**Reproduction:** The 3 to 7 dozen eggs are laid, probably in early winter, beneath rocks or logs in shallow, flowing water. Females have been found in the proximity of eggs, but it is not known whether they actually attend the clutches. Incubation seems to take 6–9 weeks. The larvae are aquatic.

**Similar Species:** The two races of the mud salamander in Florida are more slender, often have darker irises, and lack the light flecking.

**Comments:** As with most Florida salamanders, a comprehensive study of the wiles and ways of the southern red salamander is badly needed. The southern red salamander may not be as uncommon as it now seems.

## Woodland Salamander Group

# 57. Southeastern Slimy Salamander

*Plethodon grobmani*

**Size:** Adults range from 5 to 6½ inches, rarely attaining or barely exceeding 7 inches.

**Identification:** This is a slender black salamander with a variable amount of white flecking on the back and sides. The sides are usually more heavily flecked than the back. The belly is dark, but lighter than the back. A nasolabial groove is present.

**Habitat/Range:** This is a member of the woodland salamander group. Wherever pine and mixed woodlands hold even a modicum of moisture, the slimy salamander is capable of surviving. It burrows into and beneath rotting logs and mats of leaf litter and other surface debris. It also utilizes the burrows of insects and small vertebrates. This species has no aquatic larval stage. It is found in the woodlands of Florida from Tampa Bay northward throughout the state, including the entire panhandle.

**Abundance:** This salamander is locally common but becomes very difficult to find during times of drought.

**Behavior:** As do all woodland salamanders, *P. grobmani* hides persistently by day, emerging from its lair to forage at night. It often sits with only the head and shoulders out of the burrow awaiting the approach of an insect, spider, or worm.

**Reproduction:** The 8–24 eggs are laid in the interior of or beneath a rotting log, or beneath moisture-holding debris. The nesting site must remain moist but not wet. Direct development occurs, with the larvae remaining in the egg capsule until metamorphosis is completed. Nesting has been observed in the spring, incubation takes about 12–15 weeks, and the female usually remains with the clutch throughout the incubation period.

**Similar Species:** The mole salamander is the closest in color to the slimy salamander; however, the mole salamander is short, stocky, and brownish rather than black, has a proportionately large head, and lacks the nasolabial groove.

**Comments:** The slimy salamander complex consists of at least 16 species of biochemically distinct, largely look-alike salamanders. Of these, only *P. grobmani* occurs in Florida.

The slimy salamanders are named for their copiously exuded, cloying skin secretions that are actually more glutinous than slimy.

## WATERDOGS (MUDPUPPIES): FAMILY PROTEIDAE

This family is represented by only one species in Florida, which is restricted to streams in the panhandle. It is usually referred to as a waterdog, but is occasionally called a mudpuppy.

At the moment, its taxonomy is uncertain, so future texts may refer to the same species by both different common and scientific names.

Waterdogs have only 4 toes on each foot and, as permanent neotenes, retain external gills and lack eyelids throughout their lives.

## Dogs—Waterdogs, That Is—in a Florida Creek

It was a sunny weekend in North Florida. Having nothing better to do (is there ever anything better than getting out into the field?), Patti and I decided to take a drive from our home in Lee County up to the Apalachicola National Forest in the panhandle. We had recently learned that a species of waterdog (mudpuppy, if you will) dwelt in some of the Panhandle's creeks, and there would never be a better time to check out a population or two for ourselves.

Among the salamanders, skulkers all, the waterdogs are professional skulkers, so it was with some trepidation that I viewed our possible success; Patti was more certain that we would succeed. Even I agreed that it would be a nice trip—a pleasant few days away from the hustle and bustle of everyday life.

When it was first found that waterdogs actually occurred in Florida, it was thought that two species were involved. The Florida panhandle was thought to be the southernmost extension of the range of the mobile dwarf waterdog, *Necturus punctatus lodingi*, as well as where the range of the easternmost population of the Gulf Coast waterdog, *N. beyeri*, terminated. Later it was realized that the range of the dwarf waterdog extended no farther south than central Georgia; by default, the Florida panhandle waterdogs all became Gulf Coast waterdogs.

That belief remained until genetic comparisons of all waterdogs and mudpuppies of the Gulf Coast states were made about fifteen years ago, when two long-held beliefs were disproven. First, the Alabama waterdog was found to be a very different creature than the Gulf Coast waterdog with which it had long been lumped, and, second, the populations of "Gulf Coast waterdog" east of Mobile Bay were found to differ genetically from those west of the bay. From that point, on the Florida animals were an undescribed species, and a change was suggested for both its common and scientific names. Rather than Gulf Coast waterdog, the common name became Eastern Gulf Coast waterdog, and the scientific terminology was changed to *Necturus* species cf *beyeri*. This indicates that the creature is an undescribed species and seems most closely allied with *N. beyeri*. Sadly, the 15-year study stopped short of redescribing the population east of Mobile Bay, and the project has not yet been picked up again.

*continued*

But now back to *our* trip. Patti and I drove around in the forest for a while before deciding to try our luck in a hip-deep stream about 10 feet wide. The water ran over a little riffle, then swirled and puddled at the edges as it continued through a deeper pool. On the pool bottom lay a profusion of fallen limbs, and at the distant end, a hefty pack of fallen, now sodden leaves.

As we sorted carefully through the first netful of leaves, we found myriad aquatic insects and a half-dozen larvae of the southern two-lined salamander. The next netful and the next brought up more of the same.

Certain there were more leaf packs, we moved upstream a bit and found another. The very first netful of leaves brought up two examples of the sought species—a 3-inch and a 4-inch Eastern Gulf Coast waterdog.

It would have been a beautiful day and a wonderful interlude even had we failed, but success in finding these professional skulkers made the trip ever so much more memorable.

# 58. Eastern Gulf Coast Waterdog

*Necturus* species cf *beyeri*

**Size:** This is a small waterdog. Adults vary from 5 to 7 inches in total length but occasionally exceed 8 inches.

**Identification:** The eastern Gulf coast waterdog is clad in mud tones dorsally and laterally and is profusely marked with obscure to well-defined rounded dark spots of moderate size. These are usually more visible on the sides than on the back. The venter is light and unspotted. The gills are bright red. Immatures are similar to the adults in appearance.

**Habitat/Range:** These salamanders prefer streams of small to moderate size with a fair current. Waterdogs can be common where cover in the form of snags and leaf beds is adequate. These waterdogs range from Leon and Wakulla counties westward.

**Abundance:** Common, especially in smaller sizes, in panhandle streams.
**Behavior:** This is a secretive aquatic species of salamander. They are stream dwellers and can be common in areas where bottom detritus accumulates. They are most often seen in the winter and early spring months.
**Reproduction:** We must again state, as with so many others, that little is known about the life history or reproductive biology of this salamander. In Alabama, nests containing 37–67 eggs have been reported for a species of similar size. It is probable that the eastern Gulf coast waterdog is a winter breeder that lays its clutch in the spring beneath tree roots, sunken logs, or similarly protected areas.
**Similar Species:** This is the only large aquatic salamander in Florida having only 4 toes on all 4 feet.
**Comments:** As of 2010, this Florida waterdog has not been formally described.

---

## NEWTS: FAMILY SALAMANDRIDAE

Just as all toads are frogs, but not vice versa, all newts are salamanders, but not all salamanders are newts. In Florida this family of largely more northerly salamanders is represented by only two species, one with two subspecies. The more specialized of the two, the striped newt, has been declining in numbers for some time and is now locally distributed and uncommon. The two subspecies of red-spotted newts (the peninsula and the central newts) are common to abundant.

Although as adults newts are capable of emerging from the water, in many areas of Florida they are aquatic their entire long lives. In some areas, newts are neotenic; that is, they attain sexual maturity but fail to assume other adult characteristics. Perhaps the most noticeable of these characteristics is retention of the external gills.

Because the peninsula and central newts are rather easily found at all stages of their lives, their natural histories are fairly well known—at least compared with the lives of many other salamanders, including the congeneric striped newt.

In ideal conditions, the life of the eastern newts is divided into four stages: the aquatic egg stage, the aquatic larval stage, the terrestrial eft stage (this may be skipped if terrestrial conditions are hostile), and the adult stage, which is aquatic in the subspecies of the red-spotted newt and either aquatic or terrestrial (depending on whether their ponds hold water) in the striped newt.

Adult newts have rough skin; the skin of the larvae is smooth and slimy. During the breeding season, males develop heightened tailfins and black, roughened excrescences on the inner sides of the hind legs and on the toe tips. These help the male retain a breeding embrace with

## To Newt or Not to Newt, That Is the Question

On several mornings I had contemplated driving southward a bit into Marion County to search for red-striped newts, but one thing or another had come up, and I never went. Then one day Kim Sash (and her big yellow lab, Miles), Pierson Hill, and Kenny Wray decided they'd like go newting and invited me to accompany them. This time I went. I think Kim and Pierson just wanted to see the red-striped newts again, but Kenny hoped to find a metamorphosed adult for pictures. Finding adults can be tough at best of times.

It was a beautiful, clear day, the pond water was just on the comfortable side of tepid, tadpoles were abundant, "alligator fleas" (some dastardly hemipteran insect with a propensity to bite any endotherm it bumped into!) were uncomfortably abundant, but worse than the bug bites, we were having a tough time finding newts. Even the usually rather common paedomorphic form was playing hard to get on that day.

Finally our luck turned a bit. Pierson got one or two large-sized paedomorphs, Kenny got a couple, and even I, with a small net, managed to get one or two. Findings of interesting insects, big leeches, and little centrarchid fish as well as those tadpoles kept our interest level up all day.

As it neared time to leave, Kenny and I decided to walk the circumference of the pond. Kenny was working the shoreline hard with his custom net, and I was a few feet from the shoreline in a couple feet of water. Our walk had produced only another two or three paedomorphic newts, but just as we were about to leave the water, the pond, and the area, Kenny hollered out, "Got one!" Got what? I asked.

Got a young adult—no gills, nice stripes, real pretty, was Kenny's response. A nice day had just become a great day.

the female. The female is grasped around her neck or shoulders by the "nonskid" hind legs of the male. Tail undulations by the male apparently waft stimulatory pheromones to the female. After adequate stimulation, she will pick up a sperm packet from the tip of a spermatophore with her cloacal labia. Following this the eggs are laid singly and often loosely wrapped in the leaf of an aquatic plant.

# 59. Striped Newt

*Notophthalmus perstriatus*

**Size:** This slender salamander is adult at 2¾ inches, rarely attaining a total length of 3½ inches.

**Identification:** Adults are yellowish green, olive, or nearly brown dorsally. Cold specimens are usually darker than warm ones. The red dorsolateral stripes that give this newt its name begin on the head and continue uninterruptedly (occasionally with minor interruptions) to about halfway down the tail, where they then break into a series of dashes. There may be a series of poorly defined red dashes below the red stripe. The red stripes and dashes may be partially and narrowly edged with black. The yellow belly bears a few black spots. During the aquatic breeding season, a rather large tail fin and black excrescences on the inner sides of the hind legs develop. Neotenic striped newts may lack all indications of striping.

**Habitat:** The distribution of this pretty species is enigmatic even to researchers. It can be fairly common in one situation but rare or absent from several nearby areas that seem virtually identical. Look for the striped newt in and near temporary ponds and cypress heads in pine flatwoods and the pine-dominated sandhill areas of north Florida. It may be found locally in the northern two-fifths of the peninsula and the easternmost region of the panhandle.

**Abundance:** This is now an uncommon (and apparently still declining) species.

**Behavior:** Much of the life history of the striped newt remains steeped in mystery. Males have been seen amplexing gravid females in late March. Numbers of efts have been found near breeding ponds during and following hard rains. Adults have been found beneath fallen limbs and logs near dried ponds. The strategy used by these newts to avoid desiccation in well-drained habitats is not known.

**Reproduction:** Little is known with certainty about the reproductive biology of the striped newt. It is known to be a spring breeder. Newly hatched larvae have been found from late March through April. It is thought that metamorphosis occurs in about 8 months, although paedomorphic populations are widespread and common. Where and when terrestrial conditions are hostile, the eft stage may be bypassed.

**Similar Species:** No other newt or salamander in Florida has a continuous or nearly continuous red stripe along each side.

# 60. Central Newt

*Notophthalmus viridescens louisianensis*

**Size:** Although most central newts are adult at 2¾–3½ inches in length, some may attain 4 inches.

**Identification:** This is a pretty little newt. The dorsum is yellow green to dark olive. The dorsal skin is granular and rather rough. A dorsolateral row of tiny red spots is often present on each side; these are usually not edged with black. The yellowish belly is heavily peppered with tiny black spots. Breeding males develop wide tail fins.

When conditions allow, the terrestrial eft stage does occur, but the colors are not significantly brighter than those of the adults.

**Habitat:** Central newts can be found in most upland canals, lakes, ponds, and drainage ditches over the northern one-fifth of the Florida peninsula and the entire panhandle. They also occur in the backwaters and oxbows of rivers and creeks. This newt is often associated with areas of profuse aquatic growth.

**Abundance:** This newt is a common denizen of many heavily vegetated waterholes.

**Behavior:** Because of the excessive seasonal dryness throughout much of Florida, central newts are often aquatic throughout their lives. Occasional adults may be found beneath moisture-retaining mats of water-edge vegetation or crossing roadways on rainy nights. Unlike the striped newt, which often dwells in ephemeral ponds, the various races of the red spotted newt prefer permanent sources of water.

**Reproduction:** Central newts breed in the winter and spring months. Males develop a heightened tail fin and horny, black excrescences on the inner sides of their hind legs during the breeding season. Using their hind legs, males grasp females around their neck or shoulders. Undulations of the tail fin waft stimulating pheromones to the female. After sufficient stimulation, the female picks up a sperm packet with her cloacal labia. The 50–150 (sometimes more) eggs are laid singly and placed by the female on the stems and leaves (sometimes loosely wrapped in a leaf) of a submerged plant.

**Similar Species:** None. The striped newt has continuous red stripes from nose to tail.

61. Peninsula Newt, *Notophthalmus viridescens piaropicola*, is the darkest of the four races of the red-spotted newt. The dorsum is dark olive, olive brown, or nearly black. Small black spots, heaviest laterally, may be present. There are no red dorsolateral spots. The venter is dark olive yellow, heavily peppered with fine black dots. The larvae are dark with a liberal peppering of darker spots dorsally and laterally and have a black-spotted pinkish white venter. Although they are usually fully aquatic throughout their lives, occasional adults may be found beneath moisture-retaining vegetation at water's edge or crossing rain-swept roadways. The species ranges over virtually all the southern four-fifths of the Florida peninsula.

## SIRENS: FAMILY SIRENIDAE

The salamanders in this family are so divergent from others that they were once placed in their own order, the Trachystomata.

All are fully aquatic, retaining three pairs of bushy external gills throughout their long lives. Hind limbs and pelvic girdle are lacking;

## Siren—Siren, Small and Large

Have we found it? Yes or no?

"It" is the Gulf Hammock dwarf siren, a subspecies described by Wilfred T. Neill from two groups back in the mid-1900s and then never seen again.

But just maybe we have seen it, and despite Neill's comments otherwise—that the dwarf siren shown him by Paul Moler and Barry Mansell, a siren taken from within a mile or so of the originals, by the way, was not his Gulf Hammock subspecies—just maybe the negative was more a case of faulty memory than actuality.

Because of Neill's comments, when Moler and I netted a few dwarf siren from that little Gulf Hammock roadside pond, we concluded that we still had not found the real thing.

When biologists Kenny Wray and Pierson Hill netted a few siren from the pond, not burdened by Neill's comments, they concluded that the little creatures actually were the missing Gulf Hammock subspecies. Certainly the pattern of striping, the color of the lateral striping, and the ventral pattern were correct, but it was the intensity of the pattern—an insufficient contrast between the striping and the ground color—that created the quandary.

But Wray and Hill have convinced me. Moler remains unconvinced but may be swaying a bit to the right of his steadfast "no." That this creature is the "missing" siren makes more sense than attempting to justify why it is not.

And now, for a tale about a hunt for greater siren, I defer to Patti.

There is a culvert in this town, and in it some sirens of renown . . .

One of the advantages of living in Gainesville is that wildlife is generally accessible within about a 15-minute drive, which is about as long as it takes to get out of town. On the north side of town, you head for San Felasco Hammock, a state park known for its birds and its biking and hiking trails. On the south side of town, you head for Payne's Prairie.

But if you don't feel like making the trek all the way to the prairie, there's always that drainage canal next to the Florida Fish and Wildlife Conservation Commission Office on Williston Road. The cement-lined ditch serves as an outflow from Bivens Arm, a small lake snuggled down between Main and 13th streets. The ditch is close to our house, and once or twice a month we check it out to see what's moving. Sometimes all we find are leeches, their wormlike bodies pressed against the rough cement near the water's edge,

*continued*

waiting for unwary prey such as frogs, turtles, or humans. Because of the leeches' anticoagulant saliva, a single host is enough for a feast. Other times we have seen tiny catfish wiggling like animated commas as they snorkled food items out of the cracks between canal components.

During some months of the year, the ditch is crowded with crayfish hunters when the crustaceans make their pointy-toed way from Bivens Arm to the Prairie. At other times we find siren, long eel-shaped amphibians with mucus-laden skin, prominent external gills, and no hind limbs.

We were hoping to see a greater siren as we pulled onto the right-of-way next to the ditch. Net and bucket in hand, I jumped out of the car and rushed to where the culvert emerges on the Payne's Prairie side. I turned my flashlight beam downward, between my feet.

The light played over the large black scaly back of a 12-foot alligator "fishing" the water in the culvert, mouth agape. He heard my footsteps and raised his open mouth to eye me warily. His torso seemed to fill the 4-foot-wide ditch, and his teeth looked very white.

I took an involuntary step backward and decided I'd look for siren some other time.

---

only forelimbs are present. The forelimbs, although small, are moved in a walking sequence when the siren is moving slowly on the pond or river bottom. They are folded along the side while the siren is swimming, then brought forward into "landing position" as the siren comes to rest.

The use of the colors and patterns described below for the identification of the dwarf sirens may be inconclusive in some cases. Broad overlaps and variations have now been found.

Whether pale and difficult to see or bright and obvious, the striping of the three subspecies of *Pseudobranchus striatus* is usually quite precise and rather evenly edged, whereas the stripes of the two races of *P. axanthus* have uneven edges.

The dwarf sirens (*Pseudobranchus*) have only 3 toes on each forefoot and a single gill opening on each side. The members of the genus *Siren* have 4 toes on each forefoot and 3 gill slits on each side.

The breeding biology of the sirens remains nearly as muddy as the preferred habitats of most. It is thought that egg fertilization is external.

External fertilization would certainly be workable in the members of the genus *Siren*, all of which apparently lay their eggs in clumps or clusters. It seems far less efficient—in fact, almost unworkable—in the case of the two species of *Pseudobranchus*, the dwarf sirens, which are, apparently, egg-scatterers.

All sirens of both genera survive the drying of their ponds by burrowing (sometimes rather deeply) into the mud and by forming cocoons comprising one layer of slime (short droughts) to many (lengthy droughts) to conserve body moisture.

Ongoing studies have disclosed several potential species in the genus *Siren* awaiting description.

# 62. Narrow-striped Dwarf Siren

*Pseudobranchus axanthus axanthus*

**Size:** This is a tiny, slender salamander that is adult at between 5 and 8 inches in length. Very occasional specimens slightly exceed 9 inches.

**Identification:** This is a dusky-colored siren with obscure striping. A series of 4 dark dorsal stripes appears on a field of olive gray to olive green. The sides are somewhat lighter, and there are two light lateral stripes. The venter has light spots. There are only 3 toes on each forefoot. The head is rather broad, and the snout of this species is more rounded than that of *P. striatus*.

The juveniles are similar to the adults in coloration.

**Habitat/Range:** The narrow-striped dwarf siren has found ready habitat in Florida with the proliferation of the introduced water hyacinth. For at least part of the year (spring, summer, and autumn) it is easily found by dredging hyacinths and carefully sorting through their root systems. Dredging at the same sites in the winter has produced few of these salamanders. Many researchers consider this a siren of open areas—ponds, marshes, and the like. This siren occupies a range south of a line drawn from Jacksonville to Gulf Hammock and north of a line at the latitude of the northern edge of Lake Okeechobee.

**Abundance:** This small sirenid seems common to abundant, but only seasonally available to "traditional" collecting methods.

**Behavior:** This is a very secretive, fully aquatic salamander. It seems inactive by day but does forage among the hyacinths, frogsbit, and water lettuce roots, or through the bottom detritus, by night. Additional studies into the life histories and genetics of all populations of dwarf sirens are badly needed.

**Reproduction:** Much regarding the reproductive biology of this siren remains conjectural. It is thought that this species scatters its dozen or so eggs singly through plant material. How fertilization is accomplished is unknown.

**Similar Species:** The greater and lesser sirens have 4 toes on each hand. See accounts 64, 65, and 66 for a discussion of the very similar *P. striatus*.

**Comments:** Dwarf sirens of both species are coveted bass baits in central Florida, although this use is seen less frequently today than a decade ago.

63. Everglades Dwarf Siren, *Pseudobranchus a. belli*, is the more contrastingly patterned, smaller, southern subspecies. This 4–6-inch siren ranges southward from the latitude of northern Lake Okeechobee to the southern tip of the peninsula. Its venter is a nearly unicolored gray; the lateral stripe is buff, bordered on both top and bottom by a light stripe; the dorsum is dark (olive black) and contains three lighter stripes. This southern subspecies is more difficult to find than the northern race. In our many hours of seining in the creeks and canals of southern Florida, we have found only a few examples.

# 64. Broad-striped Dwarf Siren

*Pseudobranchus striatus striatus*

Slender
Broad-striped
Gulf Hammock

**Size:** This dwarf siren attains a length of about 8 inches.

**Identification:** This race has a dark back bordered by a rather broad light line on each side. A poorly defined, narrow vertebral line is present.

Often difficult to discern, a narrow light lateral line is present on each side. The belly is rather prominently reticulated or mottled.

**Habitat/Range:** Acidic cypress pools and swamps in pine flatwoods are the preferred habitat of this salamander. It is found more often in the muck and detritus of pond bottoms than in floating vegetation. This is the most northeasterly race of the 3 subspecies. It ranges southward from southeastern South Carolina to extreme northeastern Florida.

**Abundance:** Rather than being rare, it seems probable that it is the secretive habits of this persistent burrower that make it difficult to find.

**Behavior:** The slender dwarf siren is an accomplished burrower in pond bottom detritus. Should their pond dry up, they are capable of burrowing deeply and secreting a moisture-conserving slime cocoon. Although this siren has reproduced in captivity, the breeding sequence was not witnessed.

**Reproduction:** This siren is believed to be an egg scatterer, but virtually nothing is known with certainty.

**Similar Species:** See species accounts 62 and 63 for a discussion of the very similar narrow-striped dwarf siren. The lesser and greater sirens both have 4 toes on each forefoot.


65. Gulf Hammock Dwarf Siren, *Pseudobranchus striatus lustricolus*. It appears that the enigma of the Gulf hammock dwarf siren, long thought lost to science, has been clarified. Despite knowledge of precise locales from which it originally came, its whereabouts had been unknown for more than 50 years. In the 1950s both adult and hatchling specimens were collected and described from a group of siren found in hurricane-flooded roadside ditches and overflow ponds in the Gulf Hammock area (Citrus and Levy counties) of northwestern peninsular Florida. It was from these specimens that the subspecies was described.

According to the original description, this 8-inch dwarf siren was the most distinctively and contrastingly marked of the group. As described, the broad, dark dorsal stripe contained three precisely defined yellowish stripes. In addition, an orange buff dorsolateral and a silvery gray ventrolateral stripe appeared on each side. The belly was dark. The collection data were a bit erroneous, but they definitely got researchers into the range of this subspecies.

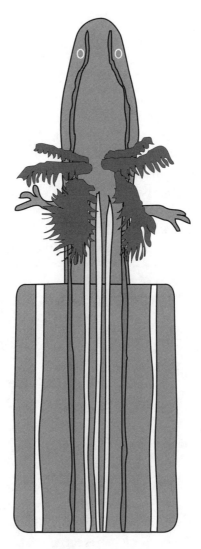

Gulf Hammock siren

For more than 50 years several researchers had scoured the published locales and had even found dwarf sirens within a few feet of the published type locale, but the somewhat "hazy" appearance of the siren found did not seem to quite fit the description. The colors were fine, but the pattern clarity seemed somewhat compromised.

Finally, after more than a half a century of color and pattern comparisons it has been decided that the specimens in question actually were (and are) the Gulf Coast dwarf siren, and also that the subspecies, if valid as described, is somewhat more variable than initially thought.

66. Slender Dwarf Siren, *Pseudobranchus striatus spheniscus*. The slender dwarf siren is the most pallid and, at an adult length of 4–6 inches, the most diminutive of the *P. striatus* group. The dark middorsal field contains three rather poorly defined buff stripes. At each side of the dark vertebral area is a somewhat better defined light (yellowish) stripe, below which are an olive stripe and a yellowish lateral stripe. The venter is gray(ish) with irregularly placed obscure light spots. There are only 3 toes on each forefoot. The head is narrow, and the snout is wedge shaped.

This subspecies ranges northward from the latitude of Orlando to southern Georgia.

# 67. Eastern Lesser Siren

*Siren intermedia intermedia*

**Size:** The eastern lesser siren is adult at from 8 to about 20 inches. Lengths greater than 12 inches seem quite uncommon.

**Identification:** In Florida, most lesser sirens are brown, bluish brown, black, or bluish black. The spots, if present, are dark rather than light. A light-colored "mustache" is often present. The tail tip is rather narrowly pointed. Juveniles may be dark olive green or olive black but also have dark spots. The hatchlings may have a red(dish) band on the sides of the head and across the top of the head. Lesser sirens have prominent external gills and 4 toes on the front feet, and the rear legs are lacking.

**Habitat/Range:** Slow rivers, ditches, canals, cypress ponds, and reservoirs are among the habitats utilized by this eclectic salamander. Small specimens are often found in mats of hydrilla, hydrocotyl, frogsbit, and the roots of water lettuce and water hyacinth. It is found in most of mainland Florida but is apparently absent from the Everglades.

**Abundance:** This is a common salamander that inhabits vegetation-choked waterways.

**Behavior:** This is a secretive burrower that seems to shun open water situations. It may occasionally be seen foraging at night in muddy and/or vegetated shallows. If the lesser siren's waterhole dries up, the salamander burrows deeply into the mud and creates a multilayered slime cocoon that prevents desiccation. Lesser sirens live well in aquaria and are interesting and easily cared for.

**Reproduction:** Knowledge of the breeding biology of this and other sirens remains fraught with uncertainties. Brooding females have been found. One found in a southwest Florida canal was attending a nest of 206 eggs; another guarded 381 eggs. The nests were about 12 feet from shore, on peat mats, beneath coverings of water hyacinths.

**Similar Species:** Adults of the greater siren are much larger than adults of the lesser siren. Greater siren can typically be ruled out by the presence of light dorsal and lateral flecking; however, some greater siren do have dark flecking and identification can be confusing. Dwarf sirens retain stripes throughout their lives and have only 3 toes on their forefeet.

**Comments:** The western lesser siren, *Siren intermedia nettingi*, is found almost to the Alabama-Florida state line. This larger (to 20 inches) and more prominently spotted race may eventually be found in the Escambia drainage of Florida's western panhandle. The western lesser siren has light spots on its belly. Hatchling western lesser siren have a light vertebral stripe and a light ventrolateral stripe on each side.

# 68. Greater Siren

*Siren lacertina*

**Size:** The greater siren is the second longest of Florida's salamanders but may actually be the largest by weight. Adult greater sirens range from

24 to 30 inches in total length and may occasionally exceed 36 inches. Although elongate, they are of robust build.

**Identification:** The ground color of the greater siren varies from brown to olive green both dorsally and ventrally. The lower sides may be somewhat lighter than the dorsum. The back may be mottled with spots or bars of darker pigment. The sides are flecked with gold, blue, green, or black. Old, large specimens may be duller than younger animals. The external gills arc prominent. The forelimbs are well developed and used in a walking motion when the siren moves slowly along the pond bottom. Each forefoot has 4 toes. The eyes lack lids. As with all sirens, rear limbs are lacking.

Hatchlings and juveniles have prominent light vertebral and lateral stripes and light chin, cheeks, and venter.

When nonregenerated, the compressed tail tip of the greater siren is rather bluntly rounded in profile.

**Habitat/Range:** The greater siren utilizes a variety of habitats. Although the adults may utilize open water situations, they are also found amid the snags, hydrilla, and spatterdock of Florida's drainage canals. Look for these salamanders in ponds, lakes, slow rivers, canals, water-filled ditches, and any permanent and semipermanent bodies of water. Hatchlings and juveniles are commonly found in mats of floating aquatic vegetation.

**Abundance:** The greater siren is common in rivers, canals, drainage ditches, and other such areas throughout the state of Florida (excepting the Keys).

**Behavior:** This is a fully aquatic salamander that is often quiescent by day but actively forages under cover of darkness. It may also be active on cloudy days and during periods of low barometric pressure. Greater sirens are often caught by fishermen and generally unjustly feared. Sirens bury deeply into pond-bottom mud, create a moisture-retaining, multilayered slime cocoon, and become dormant when their ponds dry.

**Reproduction:** Virtually nothing is known about the reproductive biology of this interesting salamander. It is speculated that breeding occurs in late winter, that egg fertilization is external, and that the several hundred eggs are deposited in shallow water situations. Larval greater siren less than 2 inches long have been found in the early spring in north Florida and in late winter in south Florida.

**Similar Species:** In Florida the lesser siren tends to have a bluish cast to its brown body, dark spots on the side, and a much more sharply pointed tail tip.

**Comments:** This species reportedly makes "plaintive yelping sounds" when disturbed. If properly cared for, greater sirens will live for decades in an aquarium.

**3**

# Peripheral Amphibian Species

One frog (the pickerel frog) and two salamander species (the spotted salamander and the three-toed amphiuma) are known to occur only a few miles north and/or west of the Florida state line in Alabama. Additionally, the range of the western lesser siren, a subspecies of the eastern lesser siren, nears the Escambia River near the state's western border. The former three are discussed here. The western lesser siren is discussed in Comments in species account 67, the eastern lesser siren.

## 69. Pickerel Frog

*Rana palustris*

**Size:** Although occasional females attain 3½ inches SVL, males and most females are an inch or so shorter.

**Identification:** Pickerel frogs usually have paired, rectangular or square brown spots between the light-colored dorsolateral ridges and another row of large spots beneath the ridges. In some cases there may be three rows of spots, especially posteriodorsally, and smaller spots beneath the large lateral ones. The spots may coalesce into bars or stripes. The ground color is tan or light brown. The venter is white (sometimes smudged with dark pigment) but suffused with bright yellow or orange in the groin and on the concealed surfaces of the hind legs. Juveniles are less colorful ventrally than adults.

Proportionately, the bilateral external vocal sacs of this ranid are rather small.

The tadpoles are greenish to greenish brown dorsally, lighter (off-white to cream yellow) ventrally, and have grayish fins smudged with patches of darker pigment.

**Voice:** The low-pitched rolling snore of male pickerel frogs is produced either above or beneath the water surface. North of Florida, pickerel frogs vocalize on cool spring evenings, often in conjunction with peepers and American toads.

**Habitat/Range:** North of Florida, pickerel frogs are associated with both cool woodland ponds and streams and the warmer, more silted waters of the coastal plain. It is suspected that if pickerel frogs do occur in Florida, they will be found in the streams associated with the cooler ravines of the extreme western panhandle.

**Abundance:** If the pickerel frog exists (or existed) in Florida, it was and is one of the state's rarest frogs. Although records are questioned by some biologists, Florida museum specimens have reportedly come from the Pensacola area.

**Behavior:** Although it occasionally wanders afield in damp weather, the pickerel frog seems quite closely associated with water at all times of year. It is agile and alert; when startled, it may make several leaps before stopping.

**Reproduction:** In Florida, details of the reproductive biology of the pickerel frog are unknown. Elsewhere, the eggs, which may number several thousand, are laid in one or more clumps. Each clump is attached to subsurface (often bottom) vegetation such as sticks or grasses. Males call while submerged, while floating, while sprawling atop or clinging to floating vegetation, or while sitting in water-edge grasses.

**Similar species:** Other than a vague possibility of finding a pickerel frog in Escambia County, any spotted frog encountered in Florida will be a leopard frog or a gopher frog (see accounts 27, 33, and 34). Gopher frogs have spots of irregular outline and are squat and almost toadlike in appearance. Leopard frogs have rounded or oval spots.

**Comments:** Pickerel frogs have fairly toxic skin secretions. Other frog species housed with pickerel frogs usually rapidly succumb. Although you should wash your hands after handling any amphibian or reptile, it is a particularly good idea to do so after handling pickerel frogs, river frogs, giant toads, Cuban treefrogs, or newts.

# 70. Spotted Salamander

*Ambystoma maculatum*

**Size:** Most adults range from 5½ to 7 inches in total length. Occasional specimens are known to exceed 8½ inches.

**Identification:** The spotted salamander is black(ish) dorsally and gray ventrally. There is usually a double row of yellow to orange spots (sometimes orange on the head and yellow on the back) dorsally. Rarely the namesake spots may be absent or unevenly scattered. Light blue flecks occur on the sides. The metamorphs have confusingly fragmented dorsal patterns but assume normal markings within a few days.

**Habitat:** The spotted salamander is associated with hardwood forests and woodlands. It breeds in ephemeral ponds and puddles.

**Abundance:** The spotted salamander is usually seen for only a few days each year during breeding migrations or its presence in breeding ponds. It can be locally common. Since the species has been found in Alabama virtually to the Florida state line (Escambia County), it is possible that it will eventually be found in the Sunshine State.

**Behavior:** Except during the few days of the year when they are in breeding puddles, spotted salamanders are persistent burrowers. They are occasionally found beneath ground litter (logs or rocks) during periods of wet weather, when induced to move upward; however, this is the exception rather than the norm.

**Reproduction:** The spotted salamander is a winter breeder. It is stimulated to move above ground and into breeding migrations by heavy rains (often those associated with a warm front) that moderate winter temperatures or break a drought. Males usually arrive at a pond first and deposit spermatophores (stalked sperm packets) on pond-bottom litter such as leaves, sticks, and flat stones. Milling masses of males vie for the choicest deposition sites. The females, which arrive later, pick up the sperm packets with the cloacal labia then deposit their egg masses on submerged sticks, heavy grasses, or similar subsurface mounts. From 65 to more than 150 eggs are in a mass.

Depending on water temperature, eggs may take longer than a month to hatch, and development of the larvae can take from about 65 days to nearly twice that.

**Similar species:** The eastern tiger salamander, now an uncommon species in Florida, is larger and has variably shaped spots and an irregular pattern. The lower sides and belly of the tiger salamander are often largely olive to yellowish.

**Comments:** Eddy Brown has just informed me that he has found this salamander in Florida; however, a voucher specimen was not collected. The spotted salamander is a member of the family Ambystomatidae. For general comments on this family, see page 130.

# 71. Three-toed Amphiuma

*Amphiuma tridactylum*

**Size:** Slightly smaller than its two-toed relative, the three-toed amphiuma rarely exceeds 3 feet in length.

**Identification:** The dorsum of this large aquatic salamander is brown to brownish gray. The venter is a light gray. There is a clear line of demarcation between the dorsal and the ventral colors. The snout is flattened, the eyes are lidless and nonprotuberant. There are usually 3 toes (occasionally only 2) on each of the 4 tiny feet. The whole animal tends to dull for a few days prior to shedding. At that time the eyes appear bluish.

**Habitat:** This aquatic salamander occurs in a very wide range of aquatic habitats.

**Abundance:** This species remains unknown in Florida but nears the state line in Alabama both to the west and the north of Escambia County.

**Behavior:** This is a secretive and nocturnal salamander that may be easily seen at night in shallow-water situations.

**Reproduction:** The 150 or more eggs are laid beneath matted vegetation or other such material in a shallow-water depression. The nesting season for this species seems to be between midspring and late summer.

**Similar species:** The two-toed amphiuma is very similar but usually has only 2 toes on each foot and no clear line of demarcation between dorsal and ventral colors. The one-toed amphiuma has a single toe on each foot and a convex, rather than concave snout, when seen in profile. Sirens lack rear legs and have external gills. Both these latter are common Florida residents.

**Comments:** For comments on the family Amphiumidae, see page 130.

# Glossary

**Aestivation**—A period of warm weather inactivity, often triggered by excessive heat or drought.

**Ambient temperature**—The temperature of the surrounding environment.

**Anterior**—Toward the front.

**Anus**—The external opening of the cloaca; the vent.

**Arboreal**—Tree dwelling.

**Autotomy (Autotomize)**—Breaking off of the tail, often at a weakened vertebral fracture plane. Tail regeneration is often possible.

**Brumation**—The equivalent of hibernation for poikilothermic creatures.

**Caudal**—Pertaining to the tail.

**Cirri**—Downward-projecting appendages associated with the nostrils of some male plethodontid salamanders.

**Cloaca**—The common chamber into which digestive, urinary, and re-productive systems empty and which itself opens exteriorly through the vent or anus.

**Congeneric**—Grouped in the same genus.

**Cranial crests**—The raised ridges on the top of the head of toads.

**Crepuscular**—Active at twilight.

**Deposition**—As used here, the laying of eggs or birthing of young.

**Deposition site**—Nesting site.

**Dichromatic**—Exhibiting two color phases; often sex-linked.

**Dimorphic**—A difference in form, build, or coloration involving the same species; often sex-linked.

**Direct development**—As used in regard to amphibia, complete devel-opment within the egg capsule; no free-swimming larval stage.

**Diurnal**—Active in the daytime.

**Dorsal**—Pertaining to the back or upper surface.

**Dorsolateral**—Pertaining to the upper side.

**Dorsolateral ridge**—A glandular longitudinal ridge on the upper sides of some frogs.

**Dorsum**—The upper surface.

**Ecological niche**—The precise habitat utilized by a species.

**Ectothermic**—See **poikilothermic**.

**Endemic**—Confined to a specific region.

**Endothermic**—"Warm-blooded," pertaining to an organism that produces its own body heat.

**Femur**—The part of the leg between the hip and the knee.

**Form**—An identifiable species or subspecies.

**Genus** (pl. **genera**)—A taxonomic classification of a group of species having similar characteristics. The genus falls between the next higher designation of "family" and the next lower designation of "species." Genus names are always capitalized when written.

**Gravid**—The amphibian equivalent of mammalian pregnancy.

**Gular**—Pertaining to the throat.

**Heliothermic**—Pertaining to a species that basks in the sun to thermoregulate.

**Herpetologist**—One who studies reptiles and amphibians.

**Herpetology**—The study (often scientifically oriented) of reptiles and amphibians.

**Hybrid**—Offspring resulting from the breeding of two species.

**Intergrade**—Offspring resulting from the breeding of two adjacent subspecies.

**Juvenile**—A young or immature specimen.

**Larva** (**larval**)—The aquatic immature stage of some salamanders.

**Lateral**—Pertaining to the side.

**Melanism**—A profusion of black pigment.

**Mental gland**—An often large secreting gland on the chins of some salamanders

**Metamorph**—A baby amphibian newly transformed to the adult stage.

**Metamorphosis**—Transformation from a larva to an adult by amphibians.

**Middorsal**—Pertaining to the middle of the back.

**Midventral**—Pertaining to the center of the belly.

**Monotypic**—Containing but one type.

**Nasolabial groove**—A groove between the nostril and upper lip of plethodontid salamanders.

**Nocturnal**—Active at night.

**Nominate**—The first named form.

**Ocelli**—Dark- or light-edged circular spots.

**Ontogenetic**—Age-related (color) changes.

**Oviparous**—Reproducing by means of eggs that hatch after laying.

**Papillae**—Small, fleshy nipplelike protuberances.

**Paratoid glands**—The toxin-producing shoulder glands of toads.

**Phalanges**—The bones of the toes.

**Photoperiod**—The daily/seasonally variable length of the hours of daylight.

**Poikilothermic** (also **ectothermic**)—Pertaining to an organism with no internal body temperature regulation. The old term was "cold-blooded."

**Pollywog**—A tadpole.

**Postocular**—To the rear of the eye.

**Race**—A subspecies.

**Sibling species**—Two or more similar-appearing species supposedly derived from the same parental stock; often unidentifiable in the field.

**Species**—A group of similar creatures that produce viable young when breeding. The taxonomic designation beloq genus and above subspecies. Abbreviation, sp., plural, spp.

**Subdigital**—Beneath the toes.

**Subocular**—Below the eye.

**Subspecies**—The subdivision of a species. A race that may differ slightly in color, size, scalation, or other criteria. Abbreviation, ssp.

**Subsurface**—Beneath the surface.

**Supraocular**—Above the eye.

**Supratympanal**—Above the tympanum.

**Sympatric**—Occurring together.

**Taxonomy**—The science of classification of plants and animals.

**Terrestrial**—Land-dwelling.

**Thermoregulate**—To regulate (body) temperature by choosing a warmer or cooler environment.

**Troglobitic**—Pertaining to small animals that live in caves.

**Troglodytic**—Dwelling in caves.

**Vent**—The external opening of the cloaca; the anus.

**Venter**—The underside of a creature; the belly.

**Ventral**—Pertaining to the undersurface or belly.

**Ventrolateral**—Pertaining to the sides of the belly.

**Vocal sac**—The distensible, resonating pouch of skin on the throats of male anurans.

# Acknowledgments

The success of a publication such as this is due in large part to the efforts and generosity of colleagues and friends. With this in mind, we gratefully acknowledge the comments and concerns of such biologists as David Auth, Eddy Brown, C. Kenneth Dodd, Kevin Enge, Richard Franz, Chris Gillette, Thomas Tyning, and R. Wayne VanDevender.

Karin Burns, Dennis Cathcart, Billy Griswold, Pierson Hill, Scott Cushnir, Steven Johnson, Robbie Keszey, John Lewis, Carl D. May, Dan Pearson, Nicole Pinder, Dave Sasser, Kim Sash (and Miles), Dan Scolaro, Maria Camarrilla Wray, and Kenny Wray either joined us or allowed us to join them in the field and made certain we noticed specimens that otherwise would have gone unseen.

Bill Love, Rob MacInnes, Chris McQuade, and Eric Thiss all allowed us great latitude in photographing Florida reptiles and amphibians they felt would be of interest.

Walter Meshaka shared his accrued knowledge of the introduced reptiles and amphibians of Florida, and he shepherded us into the field that we might photograph alien species in the wild. Barry Mansell provided not only field companionship, but also images of some of Florida's more difficult-to-find amphibians and reptiles.

To Paul E. Moler we owe more than just a word of thanks. Paul unstintingly shared his knowledge of the herpetofauna of Florida, offered comments and criticisms on the text, and tried to steer us to habitats where we could photograph some of Florida's more elusive amphibians and reptiles. We are truly indebted.

To the late E. Gordon Johnston who, more than 50 years ago, introduced me (RDB) to Florida and its wonderful herpetofauna, I owe a never-ending debt of gratitude.

# Bibliography and Additional Reading

The following listing contains only a few of the publications that pertain to Florida herpetology. They are, however, among the more important contributions.

Altig, Ronald. 1970. A Key to the Tadpoles of the Continental United States and Canada. *Herpetologica* 26(2): 180–207.

Ashton, R. E., Jr., S. R. Edwards, and G. R. Pisani. 1976. Endangered and Threatened Amphibians and Reptiles of the United States. Herp. Circ. no. 5. Lawrence, Kans.: Society for the Study of Amphibians and Reptiles.

Bart, Henry L., Jr., Mark A. Bailey, Ray E. Ashton, Jr., and Paul E. Moler. 1997. Taxonomic and Nomenclatural Status of the Upper Black Warrior River Waterdog. *Journal of Herpetology* 31(2): 192–201.

Bartlett, R. D. 1988. *In Search of Reptiles and Amphibians*. New York: E. J. Brill.

Bartlett, R. D., and Patricia P. Bartlett. 1996. *Frogs, Toads & Treefrogs, A Complete Pet Owner's Manual*. Hauppauge, N.Y.: Barron's Educational Series.

———. 2006. *Guide and Reference to the Amphibians of Eastern and Central North America (North of Mexico)*. Gainesville: University Press of Florida.

———. 2009. *Guide and Reference to the Amphibians of Western North America (North of Mexico) and Hawaii*. Gainesville: University Press of Florida.

Behler, John L., and F. Wayne King. 1979. *The Audubon Society Field Guide to North American Reptiles and Amphibians*. New York: Alfred Knopf.

Conant, Roger, and Joseph T. Collins. 1991. *A Field Guide to The Reptiles and Amphibians of Eastern and Central North America*. 3rd ed. Boston: Houghton Mifflin.

Crother, Brian I. (ed). 2008. *Scientific and Standard English Names of Amphibians and Reptiles of North America North of Mexico, with Comments Regarding Confidence in our Understanding, Sixth Edition*. Hammond, La.: SSAR.

Dorcas, Mike, and Whit Gibbons. 2008. *Frogs and Toads of the Southeast*. Athens: University of Georgia Press.

Duellman, William E., and Albert Schwartz. 1958. Amphibians and Reptiles of Southern Florida. Gainesville: Bulletin of the Florida State Museum, No. 3.

Elliott, Lang. 1992. *The Calls of Frogs and Toads, Eastern and Central North America* [audio tape]. Ithaca, N.Y.: Lang Elliott Nature Sound Studio.

Elliott, Lang, Carl Gerhardt, and Carlos Davidson. 2009. *The Frogs and Toads of North America (with CD of Calls)*. New York: Houghton Mifflin.

Godley, J. Steve. 1983. Observations on the Courtship, Nests and Young of *Siren intermedia* in Southern Florida. *American Midland Naturalist*: 215–219.

Halliday, Tim, and Kraig Adler, eds. 1986. *The Encyclopedia of Reptiles and Amphibians*. New York: Facts on File.

Mitchell, Joe, and Whit Gibbons. 2009. *Salamanders of the Southeast*. Athens: University of Georgia Press.

Moler, Paul E. 1990. A Checklist of Florida's Amphibians and Reptiles (Revised). Tallahassee: Florida Game and Fresh Water Fish Commission.

Moler, Paul E., ed. 1992. *Rare and Endangered Biota of Florida*, Volume III. *Amphibians and Reptiles*. Gainesville: University Press of Florida.

Neill, Wilfred T. 1951. *A New Subspecies of Salamander, Genus Pseudobranchus, from the Gulf Hammock Region of Florida*. Silver Springs, Fla.: Ross Allen's Reptile Institute.

Reno, Harley W., Frederick R. Gehlbach, and R. A. Turner. 1972. Skin and Aestivational Cocoon of the Aquatic Amphibian, *Siren intermedia. Copeia* 1972(4): 625–631.

Schwartz, Albert, and Robert W. Henderson. 1991. *Amphibians and Reptiles of the West Indies*. Gainesville: University Press of Florida.

Wilson, Larry David, and Louis Porras. 1983. *The Ecological Impact of Man on the South Florida Herpetofauna*. Lawrence: University of Kansas.

Wright, A. H., and A. A. Wright. 1949. *Handbook of the Frogs and Toads*, 3rd ed. Ithaca, N.Y.: Comstock

# Online Resource

http://caudata.org

# Index

R. D. Bartlett is a veteran herpetologist/herpetoculturist with more than 40 years' experience in writing, photographing, and educating people about reptiles and amphibians. He is the author of numerous books on the subject, including *Florida's Snakes: A Guide to Their Identification and Habits*, *Guide and Reference to the Amphibians of Eastern and Central North America (North of Mexico)*, and *Guide and Reference to the Amphibians of Western North America (North of Mexico) and Hawaii*.

Patricia P. Bartlett has coauthored many books with R. D. Bartlett, as well as writing *Dictionary of Sharks*. She was born in Atlanta, Georgia, but grew up chasing lizards in Albuquerque, New Mexico. She graduated from Colorado State University and moved to Florida to look for turtles and work for Ross Allen in Silver Springs. Pat has worked for Great Outdoors Publishing Company, for *Springfield* magazine, and for the Springfield Science Museum and was the first director of the Ft. Myers Historical Museum. Since moving to Gainesville she has worked as a science writer and as an Asian Studies coordinator. She maintains an avid interest in herpetology, entomology, and scientific illustration.